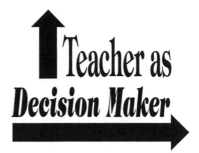
Teacher as
Decision Maker

Teacher as Decision Maker

*Real-Life Cases to Hone
Your People Skills*

Dale L. Brubaker
Lawrence H. Simon

CORWIN PRESS, INC.
A Sage Publications Company
Newbury Park, California

For information address:

Corwin Press, Inc.
A Sage Publications Company
2455 Teller Road
Newbury Park, California 91320

SAGE Publications Ltd.
6 Bonhill Street
London EC2A 4PU
United Kingdom

SAGE Publications India Pvt. Ltd.
M-32 Market
Greater Kailash I
New Delhi 110 048 India

Printed in the United States of America

Library of Congress Cataloging-in-Publication Data

Brubaker, Dale L.
    Teacher as decision maker : real-life cases to hone your people skills / Dale L. Brubaker, Lawrence H. Simon.
      p. cm.
    Includes bibliographical references (p. 180) and indexes.
    ISBN 0-8039-6081-6. — ISBN 0-8039-6082-4 (pbk.)
    1. Teachers—United States—Case studies. 2. Teaching—Case studies. 3. Education—United States—Decision making—Case studies. 4. Interaction analysis in education—Case studies. 5. Interpersonal relations—Case studies. I. Simon, Lawrence Howard, 1944–   . II. Title.
    LB1775.2.B78 1993   93-13917
    371.1—dc20   CIP

93 94 95 96 97 10 9 8 7 6 5 4 3 2 1

Corwin Press Production Editor: Yvonne Könneker

CONTENTS

FOREWORD

This is a remarkable book, for at least three reasons. First, in an extraordinarily clear fashion the writers help the reader—especially the beginning teacher or one in a preparatory program—to understand the nature and significance of certain dichotomies, for example, essentialism versus progressiveness. The writers do not bandy these labels around but specify what each of these labels means in terms of a large variety of classroom, school, and evaluation regularities. And they do this without resorting to jargon, always emphasizing the concrete rather than the abstract.

The second reason I regard this book so favorably is how sensitively—and again so clearly—Professors Brubaker and Simon describe the phenomenology of the teacher: the contradictions every teacher confronts and has to resolve in one or another way, and the scores on scores of decisions every teacher makes in the course of a single day. You cannot read these chapters and continue to talk in generalizations about how teachers think and act. There is nothing wrong with generalizations (e.g., "Teaching is rough stuff"), except when they drain concrete experience of its blood; or, as is too frequently the case, they can serve as no guide to practical action.

But without question the third reason is the most important of all because Professors Brubaker and Simon not only collected instances of very frequent or demanding cases that teachers will predictably experience, but then field-tested these instances with diverse groups of teachers in different parts of the country, all for the purpose of determining if and how these cases could be used in the preparation of teachers. I have no doubt that they have come up with a procedure derived from and embedded in a way of thinking that will be of great value to teachers, and teachers of teachers.

The writers are not dogmatists or idealogues. That, I hasten to add, does not mean they are indifferent eclectics who too easily overlook or downplay different points of view. The writers leave no one in doubt where they stand on the most important educational issues of the day. But they do not do this polemically or lopsidedly. If any adjectives are appropriate for this book they are "fair" and "balanced."

I congratulate the writers for pointing us in new directions in regard to the preparation of educators. I view the educational scene as an unintended disaster, generally speaking. Occasionally, my days are brightened when I read something that illuminates an issue, or points us in new directions, that is, something from which I can truthfully say I learned something. This, I assure the reader, is one of those "somethings."

SEYMOUR B. SARASON
Professor of Psychology Emeritus
Yale University

PREFACE

Unlike law and medicine, teacher education has no distinctive pedagogy (Shulman, 1992). In our effort to address this problem, we have one major interest: The learning of teachers must actively involve them in activities that will help them hone their people skills. Why are people skills so important to the teacher? We are reminded that success as a college student is dramatically different from success as a teacher. A college graduate describes the shift from the culture of higher education to the culture of the work world:

> In college I used my intellectual skills to get good grades by knowing the right answers. But at work, I found out that knowing the right answer was only 10 percent of the battle. Working with people was the other 90 percent. And we hadn't learned that at school. (McCall, Lombardo, & Morrison, 1988, p. 22)

We discovered that real-life cases (critical incidents) can be used to stimulate teachers to make informed decisions that can have a lasting effect on how they attempt to help children learn. Case-based teacher education can be collaborative, once teachers move past their reluctance to talk about their own "failures" and in fact get in the spirit of celebrating problems facing them in the classroom and school (Shulman, 1992).

Teacher as Decision Maker: Real-Life Cases to Hone Your People Skills was written as a valuable guide to teachers and would-be teachers. It is important to note that the book is a "guide" rather than a "manual"; "a teacher's style must utilize instruction that is inherently gratifying, and that permits self-expression" (Rubin, 1985, p. 169). This is consistent with a vision for schools and schooling that nurtures the curiosity all humans have from their earliest days (Sarason, 1993).

Prospective teachers can use cases to empathize with those who have actually been confronted with teaching situations. Future teachers can see that there is no single "right" answer to any one teaching situation, thereby taking into account the many variables involved in being a teacher. Finally, would-be teachers can use cases ". . . to question certain regularities of schooling and to begin thinking of themselves as professional educators using judgment and analysis on tough problems of practice" (Sykes, 1989, p. 7).

Seasoned teachers can bring their rich and varied experiences to an analysis of the cases. They frequently recommend a casebook to student teachers so that their student teaching is grounded in a broad spectrum of challenges facing the first-year teacher. This book may also be useful in a series of staff development sessions, where both newer and veteran teachers can be drawn together in discussions. It is not hard to imagine a future in which professional literature, case conversations, case conferences, and imaginative use of technologies are an integral part of case-based instruction (Shulman, 1992).

Perhaps the most difficult challenge in using cases is to develop "intellectual structures within which to place our cases" (Sykes, 1989, p. 8). Part I of this book was written to meet this challenge. Chapter 1, "Understanding Schools," begins by describing five functions that all schools perform for clients: confinement, training, indoctrination, sorting, and providing the conditions for personal or self-development. Schools differ only as to the degree of emphasis given each function and the way in which it is performed. The second part of Chapter 1 discusses the elements of the school as a social system. Once this framework is understood, it can be applied to any school. Persons interested in schools and schooling quickly learn that a critical incident or case is always located in a particular context.

A third framework appears in Chapter 2, "Teaching as Decision Making." It gives attention to key variables in decision making and operational guidelines for decision making. A sense of vision, resources, obstacles, alternative courses of action, timing, evaluation, and the means for revising all of the concepts above are variables that must be considered by the teacher as decision maker.

"Values and Moral Development" draws from Lawrence Kohlberg's work, which demonstrates that values are at the core of the decision-making process. The final section of Chapter 2 focuses on the teacher as a creative leader. Self-appraisal exercises are included in the interest of helping the teacher know himself or herself better. The basic assumption of this section of the chapter is that self-esteem is essential to the teacher as an effective decision maker.

Part II deals with sources of conflict in the school. The introduction to Part II discusses ways in which the critical incidents or cases in the remainder of the book can be used and responded to by the reader. A philosophical framework with essentialist and progressive positions is described and explained. An approach to the resolution of more technical cases is also discussed. Chapters 3 through 6 have cases on conflict between students and teachers, teachers and teachers, administrators and teachers, and parents and teachers. Each chapter is introduced by a brief essay that sets the stage for cases that follow.

"Interviewing for a Teaching Position" is the subject of Part III. This is an interesting and practical matter for would-be teachers as well as teachers who want to move to another school or school system. Chapter 7, "Interviewer-Teacher Conflict," contains cases designed to stimulate discussion.

We would like to acknowledge several parties for their help as we wrote this book. Special appreciation is due to the several hundred teachers who responded in field-testing the cases in seminars and workshops. Kay Fuller, Lori Penry, and Becky Wells were especially helpful in this effort. *Intercultural Interactions,* by Richard W. Brislin, Kenneth Cushner, Craig Cherrie, and Mehealana Yong, was the model for the format we used in identifying responses to technical cases. We also want to thank Paul L. Tavenner, senior editor at Brown & Benchmark, for permission to use some of the cases developed for an earlier book by the senior author. Finally, Gracia A. Alkema, president of Corwin Press, Inc., provided us with suggestions that gave us a sense of the possible and the desirable when we were too close to the writing to have a clear view.

In writing this book we have adopted a creative format that invites reader participation. We would like to hear from you as to what you experienced in using the ideas in the book. Please write us at 232 Curry Hall, University of North Carolina at Greensboro, Greensboro, NC 27412. We promise a response.

DALE L. BRUBAKER
University of North Carolina, Greensboro
LAWRENCE H. SIMON
Elon College

ABOUT THE AUTHORS

Dale L. Brubaker is a Professor of Education at the University of North Carolina at Greensboro. He was an assistant professor at the University of California, Santa Barbara, and an associate professor at the University of Wisconsin, Milwaukee. He is the author or coauthor of 12 books, including *Creative Survival in Educational Bureaucracies* and *Curriculum Planning: The Dynamics of Theory and Practice*. He received his Ph.D. in Foundations of Education from Michigan State University.

Lawrence H. Simon is a Professor of Education at Elon College in North Carolina. He received his Ed.D. in Curriculum from the University of North Carolina, Greensboro. He is the author or coauthor of several articles and the director of the Elon College Teaching Fellows Program.

P A R T I

The School as a
Social System

1 UNDERSTANDING SCHOOLS

In this chapter we will discuss the importance of context—the school setting in which critical incidents or cases are located. A simple example illustrates the importance of context. Today is Field Day at your school. It is a beautiful spring day and the children and teachers are full of energy and anticipation of the sports events that will take place. Like other teachers and the principal, you are dressed in jeans and a sweatshirt. A child approaches you and exclaims, "You look so different!" You are obviously the same person, but you have dressed differently because of the context.

Within the Field Day context, there are certain expected behaviors (regularities) on the part of participants. You and the students, for example, are expected to be noisy and laugh a lot as the competition takes place. As a participant you are so involved in events that you don't think about particular behaviors and the total context very much. In this chapter we would like to have you imagine that you are ET on a space platform, looking down at events in a school of your choice (Sarason, 1971). This may be the school where you teach or a school that you attended as a child.

Five Functions of Schools

One of the first things you notice in looking down at the school is that buses and cars drive into the parking lot and discharge students at the sidewalk near the front door. The same buses and cars return to the school later in the afternoon and pick up the students. During the interim period the students spend the entire day on the school grounds, particularly in the school building itself.

Confinement is an important function schools perform for their clients. It means that a person must be in a certain place for a specified period of time, regardless of his or her personal wishes about being there. As you investigate how confinement works, you discover that the state legislature requires that students attend school for 180 days a year. The local school board interprets the state law in this particular school system to mean that no student can leave the school grounds unless accompanied by a teacher. The principal of the school that you are observing interprets this to mean that no student can leave the school grounds unless all members of a class leave for a school-sponsored activity. (After all, a teacher can't teach a class and accompany students away from the school at the same time.)

As you look down at this school from your space platform, you notice that walls within the school building are solid rather than flexible, and there are no classroom doors that open to the grounds outside the school. The architecture of the school confines students. You notice that there are four places where confinement is most difficult to enforce: the halls, the cafeteria, the gymnasium, and the grounds outside the school building.

As you observe activities during the school day, you see that students are taught skills that fall into four main areas: (a) reading, (b) writing, (c) speaking, and (d) modes of thinking. Students who quickly demonstrate their competence in these areas are given good grades, the currency of the school. *Training* is a function designed to make students more proficient in the skills they are expected to perform.

Throughout your day observing the school, you see that a person or group is influenced by another person or group to behave in certain ways without even questioning whether this is the way a person or group either wants to or should behave. Rewards are given for appropriate behavior, sanctions are applied for inappropriate behavior, and a general environment is created in which the behavior instilled becomes second nature to persons in the school.

Indoctrination is accomplished in a number of ways. The student's schedule is filled with activities designed to promote the school's goals and objectives. For example, students learn to form lines in the cafeteria and not talk in class when others are talking.

As you look down from your space platform, you observe students being sorted into different groups in the classroom, particularly when reading is taught. You also notice that most children are reluctant to leave their groups because of the comfort and security they acquire in those groups. Some of the students have given different groups names, although the teacher uses other names to describe these groups. *Sorting* is a function that gives a great deal of power to the person or persons doing the sorting. For example, at the beginning of the year you observe the principal in a somewhat agitated state. The principal is trying to categorize students by ethnic background and is not always sure how this should be done.

Providing the conditions for personal or self-development is the final function you see performed for students. You notice that adults in the school, people from the central office building and outside experts called "consultants," talk a lot about this function and have written statements that reinforce this function. School buses, for example, have the school system motto on their sides: "Children First." And the school stationery has as its letterhead "Schools Are for Children." You note, however, that the first four functions are emphasized more for they lend themselves to measurement. The school's goal for the year is to raise standardized test scores, and faculty meetings are frequently held to teach teachers how to teach for the test. You also observe that parents seem to value the first four functions more and want their children to get good grades above all else. Many teachers in the building assign good grades, even though their grade books have grades that don't average out to the good grades they assign.

One of the difficulties in performing the last function for students is that the student needs time alone to consider who he or she is in relation to who he or she would like to become. And the day is so filled with activities designed to improve test scores that there is little "alone time" for students.

After studying the school from your platform, you realize that all schools perform these five functions for their clients. They differ only as to the *degree* and *manner* in which each function is performed.

Elements of the School as a Social System

Another way to better understand schools and their regularities is by identifying the elements of the school as a social system (Loomis & Beegle, 1960). We operate in systems all the time, although we rarely call them that. For example, imagine for a moment that it is Sunday night and you have returned from a weekend vacation. Your supermarket isn't open, so you stop at a supermarket that you have never before entered. You are able to get around this new supermarket reasonably well because you have a map in your head as to where particular goods are located. Fresh fruits and vegetables will probably be to your right after you enter the door, fresh meats will be in the center of the rear of the store, and so on. We may think of these areas of the supermarket as concepts that are part of a conceptual system known as "supermarket." Knowing the concepts and how they relate to each other within the whole framework (supermarket) allows you to transfer this learning to a similar context, even though you haven't been in the setting before.

Please return to your role as ET on a space platform as you apply the elements of the school as a social system to a school of your choice.

Objectives

As noted in our discussion of the functions your school performs for clients, the stated and actual objectives in your school are at times consistent and at other times inconsistent. For example, faculty teamwork is a stated objective in this school, but an individual faculty member is rewarded at the end of each year when the Teacher of the Year award is given. However, the principal is consistent in praising in faculty meetings those teachers whose classes have high scores on standardized tests. The school goal for the year, as you remember, is to improve standardized test scores.

There will always be some distance between stated and actual objectives in a school. But it is reasonable to assume that the greater the distance between stated and actual goals, the greater the possibility for dissonance and conflict in the school. As you study the school you are observing from your space platform, you might ask, in commonsense language, "Do they walk the way they talk?"

Norms

Norms are "rules of the game" because they describe what is acceptable or unacceptable in the school you are observing. In some schools, teachers walk in and out of the supply room to get pencils, paper, pens, and other materials. In other schools, a secretary may control access to supplies by keeping the supply room door locked, so that teachers have to ask the secretary's permission to get supplies.

The teachers' lounge is interesting to observe because people tend to let their guard down there. In some schools it is the place where those who want to can complain about the administration, parents, and students. In other schools such talk is off-limits.

One principal, especially sensitive to such criticism, sent a memorandum to faculty just before Christmas, saying that faculty members could only use the faculty room one at a time.

Status Roles

As you look down from your space platform, you observe that some people seem to be deferred to and treated openly with more respect than others. For example, in one school, teacher assistants stand back while teachers always cut birthday cakes for colleagues at the end of faculty meetings. You will also probably observe that some people in the school defer to the principal in front of him or her, but use humor to criticize the principal when he or she is absent. Every social system has a "pecking order" that is interesting to study.

Power

Power may be simply defined as *control* over others. Authority is one kind of power assigned to people in the school, but influence is exerted in the informal everyday lives of people. For example, there was not enough money in the budget to buy new furniture for the old school building. The limited amount of new furniture was delivered in the summer, and custodians placed this good furniture in the rooms of those teachers who treated them best.

As you look down at the school from your space platform, it is good to remind yourself how changes in society have produced changes in schools. Positional authority no longer has the effect it once had. The family doctor, the family attorney, and the school teacher traditionally had power that was seldom questioned. In today's society people have greater access to information and expertise and want to exercise their own influence, rather than playing a more passive role in representative government. Traditional patterns associated with gender and ethnicity have been successfully challenged, and access to power for all people has been increased.

Sanctions

Rewards (positive sanctions) and penalties (negative sanctions) are obvious as you study your school from the space platform. They are used to induce compliance with the objectives and norms of the school. It is especially interesting to observe ways in which the principal of the school uses rewards and penalties in formal situations, such as faculty meetings, and informal situations, such as conversations in the hall.

Facilities

Facilities are the means used by leaders to attain objectives. They are among the first things you will observe from your space platform. Some older schools have beautiful wood floors that lend warmth to the building because they are cared for so well. In other older schools there are fewer supplies (nonhuman resources) and caretakers (human resources). The result is a building that looks neglected. In any school there will always be more desires than resources. Is this reality understood and candidly shared by leaders in the school you are observing?

Conclusion

As you read the cases in Part II, "Sources of Conflict in Schools," please remind yourself of the two frameworks presented in this chapter, both of which depend on your ability to step back and bracket yourself as if you were ET on a space platform (Peck, 1978). The five functions schools perform for their clients, and the elements of a social system, can serve as a kind of road map that provides context for particular cases.

2 TEACHING AS DECISION MAKING

The noun *teacher* in the phrase *teacher as decision maker* can be defined by a set of related terms: *instructor, facilitator, manager, mentor, evaluator,* and *professional*. These terms represent the center of the knowledge bases of teaching.

Teaching is not only varied but it is also understood in terms of the number of interactions engaged in each day. Philip Jackson (1968) discovered that teachers are engaged in as many as 1,000 interactions each day (p. 11). Jackson's research is supported by the studies on teacher decision making by Christopher M. Clark and Penelope L. Peterson (1986): On the average, "teachers make one interactive decision every 2 minutes" (p. 274). These findings simply demonstrate that the decision-making demands of classroom teaching are relatively intense (Clark & Peterson, 1986). It is also true that beginning teachers, in contrast with experienced teachers, lack structures for making sense of critical incidents. The result is a lower level of meaning for beginning teachers engaged in the decision-making process (Calderhead, 1981). Their eye is on survival.

Key Variables in Decision Making

There are certain variables that you probably consider as you teach. The first variable is knowing what you want to achieve. We sometimes refer to this as objectives, goals, desired outcomes, or a sense of vision. To fail to recognize the importance of this variable is to let outside forces dictate how you will teach. As one humorist put it, "If you don't know where you are going, any trip will do." When you combine passion with a sense of vision, you share your energy with others, who also become inspired. To remind yourself of the difference a teacher's classroom and school leadership can make, briefly list qualities of the single best and worst teachers you had in grades K-12. Our guess is that your best teacher combined a passion for what was taught with a caring attitude toward you as a person.

A second variable is resources. You, the teacher as a decision maker, know what resources are *presently* available, what resources will *probably* be available in the future, and what resources will *possibly* be available. This knowledge helps you do many of the things you want to do in spite of the finite number of resources available to you.

As a teacher who makes a countless number of decisions, you recognize existing obstacles and project into the future to make an educated guess as to which of these obstacles will continue to exist. For example, you may presently have a principal whose philosophy of teaching is at variance with your approach to teaching. However, you know that principals in your school rarely stay more than 2 years before they are "promoted" to higher grade-level schools. Confident that your teaching style is appropriate for you and good for children, you simply ride out the present principal. This example illustrates the political dimension of teaching. When defined as "the art of the possible," politics enters into any decision-making situation. This is the third variable to consider.

A fourth variable you consider in your teaching is the alternative courses of action available to reach your objectives. You may have spent much of the weekend working on a lesson plan that features small group discussion, only to find on Monday morning that the students haven't read the assigned material. You are disappointed but switch to Plan B and show a videotape that provides much of the missing information.

Timing is the fifth critical variable. What resources should you use at different times during the decision-making process? The wise decision maker will have a sensitive eye for what should occur at what time. Patience can be the most difficult thing to achieve, yet patience and hard work are keys to success. (We are reminded that the race was won by the persistent tortoise rather than the hare that ran in spurts.) Momentum with an eye on the goal makes all the difference. There are times during the teaching act when we feel that all is lost, then something happens to cause a spark in the classroom, and it turns out to be one of our best lessons.

A sixth variable deals with your evaluation of what is happening at different stages of the decision-making process. This takes a special sensitivity to both verbal and nonverbal cues from students. In one case, for example, a student suddenly erupted in a fit of anger. We discovered, by listening intently to the student after class, that his parents had announced at breakfast that they were getting a divorce. The student's eruption in class had briefly thrown off our teaching, but effective listening provided us with invaluable information about the origin of the eruption.

Finally, as a decision maker you have machinery for altering and generating new objectives, and/or courses of action, and/or timing. The plan must be firm enough to instill confidence, yet flexible enough to find new and better directions. *Praxis,* reflective action, describes this process.

Values and Moral Development

It should be obvious from the examples we have given that values are at the core of the decision-making process. We may think of values as the substructure or keelboard on a boat. All other parts of the boat depend on the strength of the keelboard for their existence. These values are often like the two-thirds of an iceberg below the surface of the water. They make a tremendous difference in relating to self and others but are not openly discussed with others, or at times even recognized by self.

As Director of the Center for Moral Education at Harvard University, Lawrence Kohlberg developed a model for moral development that owes a great deal to the writings of Émile Durkheim, a sociologist, and John Dewey, a philosopher and educator. Both Durkheim and Dewey recognized that the social sciences and education could not be value free. Kohlberg (1970) argues that "the only integrated way of thinking about the hidden curriculum is to think of it as moral education" (p. 671). Hidden curriculum refers to the less obvious things that students learn, rather than what they are expected to learn from textbooks, curriculum guides, and teachers' lesson plans.

Kohlberg's model contains three levels, each of which has three stages. The following outline demonstrates this model:

> I. Preconventional level
>> Stage 1: The punishment-and-obedience orientation
>> Stage 2: The instrumental-relativist orientation
> II. Conventional level
>> Stage 3: The interpersonal concordance or "good boy–nice girl" orientation
>> Stage 4: The "law and order" orientation
> III. Postconventional, autonomous, or principled level
>> Stage 5: The social-contract, legalistic orientation
>> Stage 6: The universal-ethical principle orientation.
>> (1975, p. 670)

The Preconventional Level

Group conventions or norms are not the primary concern of the child who is at the preconventional level. Rather the child thinks of good or bad, right or wrong in terms of the physical power who makes the rules.

At Stage 1, "The punishment-and-obedience orientation," the child tries to avoid punishment and defers to power without questioning it. Any moral order or pattern is not the child's concern; rather power in its own right is reacted to.

The child tries to instrumentally satisfy his or her own needs while only occasionally satisfying the needs of others at Stage 2, "The instrumental-relativist orientation." Human relations are viewed in marketplace terms or pragmatic terms: "I'll help you if you help me."

The Conventional Level

At this level the child is loyal to family, group, or nation and will justify the structure, order, and persons within these known frameworks.

Stage 3, "The interpersonal concordance or 'good boy–nice girl' orientation," stresses behavior that pleases others or helps them in some way, thus winning their approval. This is the first stage at which one's intentions are considered: "Isn't it nice that he or she wanted me to help?"

At Stage 4, "The 'law and order' orientation," the person is loyal to authority, fixed rules and standards, and maintenance of the social order. One does one's duty as prescribed by law and social order.

The Postconventional, Autonomous, or Principled Level

Persons at this level are interested in defining moral values and principles that have their own integrity apart from individuals and groups. At Stage 5, "The social-contract, legalistic orientation," it is recognized that different persons have different opinions and values, which require procedures in order to reconcile them. Therefore laws are important, but of equal importance is the machinery for changing laws.

Stage 6, "The universal-ethical principle orientation," advocates that right and good be defined by conscience with one's choice of ethical principles, principles such as justice and equality that are abstract in nature.

Kohlberg argues that his six stages are "hierarchical integrations," so that higher-stage thinking depends on lower-stage thinking and, furthermore, the person tends to function at the highest stage he or she prefers. He also believes that, except in times of extreme trauma, the person advances to the next step but does not move backward and never skips steps (1975, p. 670).

Kohlberg's model is useful in that your value system as a teacher places you at a particular stage at a particular time. The obvious goal is to work your way up the hierarchy so that your students have a teacher-as-leader worth emulating. When the students and you reach higher levels, a mutuality of trust and concern becomes part of the culture of the classroom and the school. The students and you find moral authority in your values, rather than constantly looking outward for approval. An interesting challenge for you as a teacher and decision maker is to try to place various participants in a particular case at one of the six stages of moral development. In meeting this challenge you and your colleagues may be engaged in a good deal of discussion.

Operational Guidelines for Instructional Decision Making

The following operational guidelines may be helpful to you as you decide what to do with the problems and dilemmas presented by the cases in the book.

Operational Guide 1. Many decision-making situations place you as a teacher in the position of choosing from several good alternatives. For example, you have identified two activities that will help you reach your goals for a science lesson: (a) a visit to the natural science museum and (b) a visit by the natural science museum curator to your classroom. You do not feel there is enough time for both activities, so you must choose either one activity or the other. If you think in extreme either/or terms, such as there is a good decision and a bad decision, you will get a bad feeling no matter which decision you make. However, if you recognize that there are two good decisions from which you may choose, you will move ahead with your teaching without feelings of guilt for making the "wrong" decision. You will sleep better at night because the way you choose to look at this curriculum decision will lead to a desirable result.

Operational Guide 2. You, the teacher, will necessarily do some things you believe you should not do and certainly would prefer not to do. You then should choose what you consider the least harmful decision to self and others. You may be unhappy about the options open to you in evaluating student progress. It is school policy that grades are to be given. The school has traditionally used class norms for such grading, which means that those who consistently receive low grades tend to have poor self-esteem. If you must use grades, you would prefer to grade on individual progress, with the aim of building self-confidence in all your students. To do this you would give special assignments tailored to the individual needs and differences of students. You know that you will probably be criticized by the administration, teachers, and some students if you pursue this different kind of grading procedure. A more drastic option open to you is not to give grades, but this could very well cost you your job. All of your options have bad features. You must find the one that is least harmful to the students and you.

Operational Guide 3. Some decision-making situations involve balancing the desirable with the undesirable. Trade-offs are made so that you can get what you want with the minimum amount of concession to what you consider to be undesirable. As a beginning teacher you may have been accustomed to freedom from constraints when you were a college student, and object to having to fill out attendance forms, late-for-class forms, demerit forms, and the like. Imagine that you decided not to fill out forms because you ranked freedom from such tasks high in your value hierarchy. When it was discovered in the administrative office that one teacher was consciously not following bureaucratic procedures, a great deal of attention would be paid to all of your behavior. Your colleagues would criticize you for not doing your share in disciplining students. Any innovation you wanted to initiate would be suspect and given a great deal of attention. You would have violated Operational Guide 3. If you had developed an efficient system for following bureaucratic requirements, such as a computer program maintained by a student or group of students, you would have had a better chance of reaching your admirable instructional goals. Rotating individuals or groups of students responsible for such record keeping could have led to improved behavior on the part of the students, because they would have "bought into" this monitoring process.

In conclusion, there are few "right" and "wrong" decisions in something as ambiguous as educational decision making. Rather, you must be adept at weighing many alternatives and making the best decisions possible in a given situation at a particular time. Those affected by your decisions will respect you for being bright and fair as you are involved in the decision-making process, even if you occasionally make what students and colleagues think is a "wrong" decision.

It is in wrestling with the ambiguity of decision making that your creative talents will surface. In using these talents you will be influencing others to identify and use their talents. This is the subject of the next section of this chapter, "The Teacher as a Creative Leader." The creative teacher's leadership extends far beyond the classroom.

The Teacher as a Creative Leader

In the closing section of this chapter, we will discuss the importance of the Greek phrase "know thyself" as an essential element in giving creative leadership to others. To help you hone your people skills we will present ideas and exercises designed to involve you in an inner journey. The basic assumption of this section of the chapter is that self-esteem depends on meaningful interactions with others and self, and self-esteem is basic to the teacher as an effective decision maker.

Interpersonal and intrapersonal relationships form the basis for your greatest joy and emotional hardship as a teacher. Your *curriculum* (what you experience as learning settings are cooperatively created) is determined by your answer to two questions: "How shall we live together?" and "How shall I live with myself?" Some of your answers to these questions will be in conflict. The ways in which you choose to relate to these contradictions will be the key to your leadership in the classroom and the school.

Contradictions

As a teacher, you experience a seemingly endless array of contradictions. That is, you are expected to somehow reconcile opposing or mixed messages. After reading the following list of contradictions, teachers were asked to create metaphors that describe best their reactions to the list. They responded, "I sometimes feel like I'm herding cats." "I feel like a juggler." "It's like steering a dog by moving its tail."

Contradictions Facing the Teacher

Professional autonomy

→ State regulation and supervision ←

"You are the professional with expertise."

→ "Outside consultants are the experts." ←

Competition with other schools

→ Cooperation with other schools ←

Display accomplishments.

→ Quietly go ahead with "business." ←

Think (plan) ahead.

→ Catch up (look backward). ←

Be positive.

→ Face the negative. ←

It is clear from teachers' responses to this exercise that contradictions are double-edged. They are often a source of consternation while at the same time a challenge that can bring out our creativity as teachers and leaders. How is this possible? Contradictions produce interior tension that awakens us from comfortable routines, traditions, and rituals. "There is a constant battle in each of us," according to psychiatrist Arnold A. Hutschnecker (1974), "between the forces of excitation and inhibition" (p. 8). And it is the contradictions that really bother us that force us to be proactive as educational leaders. A third-grade teacher describes a contradiction that caused her to lose sleep and weight:

> Each school in our system has a "report card" that tells the public our annual goal, objectives and plan of action. Our school's major goal was to raise standardized test scores. *My* class was well on its way to meeting this goal when a new student, a nonreader with low test scores, arrived on the scene from another town. My first reaction was "Why did I have to get this student? I wish he would move again!" At the same time I realized that I, a good teacher, was exactly the kind of person who could make a difference in his life.

How did the third-grade teacher reconcile this contradiction? First, she decided to do the work necessary to deal with this situation, rather than denying its reality. Without being conscious of it, she located her commitment to the child and situation at Level 5, and perhaps Level 4, on the following Commitment Scale/Hierarchy (Brubaker & Nelson, 1974, p. 102).

1. I will sacrifice my life and/or the lives of my family and/or those I dearly love;
2. I will give up the respect of those whom I love and I'll forego my status and professional achievement;
3. I will forego economic security and my career;
4. I will have serious conflicts between what I think should be done and my reluctance to do it. I may have to alter my

work style and give up those techniques which had previously been successful and beneficial and learn new ones;

5. I will have to alter some habits with which I'm quite comfortable, thus making my job somewhat more difficult. I
   will feel uncomfortable from time to time as I'll do things
   that don't seem to be the best way to do them based on my
   past experience and present assumptions;

6. It doesn't make any difference as past experience indi-
   cates. My choice, therefore, is between Tweedledee and
   Tweedledum.

Some contradictions call for hard psychological work. Others
are a cause for celebration, even though they also require different kinds of work—usually of a more technical, logistical nature.
For example, Janet and Jim are very bright students who recently joined your class. You enjoy their creative insights, but
they are so quick that you often find it hard work to create challenging assignments for them while other students plod along.
The payoff for you is that you learn more as a teacher because of
this challenge.

Please take a moment to identify those contradictions you
expect to celebrate (or do celebrate) as a teacher and those contradictions you expect will (or presently do) demand hard psychological work. Then turn to the next page to see how other teachers have completed this exercise.

Column 1	Column 2
(celebrate)	*(reconcile)*

Contradiction comes from the Latin *contra* (against) plus *dicere* or *dictus* (to say). It is defined in the dictionary as "the act of saying the opposite of something already said." Two kinds of contradictions facing the teacher are the basis for the following exercise: (1) those one chooses to celebrate and (2) those one chooses to work on to try to reconcile. Please identify contradictions you face as a leader and celebrate, and those you choose to work on to try to reconcile.

Column 1 (celebrate)	Column 2 (reconcile)
"We have excellent parent involvement and this means we give many of our resources (e.g., time and effort) to parents."	"I always feel like I'm the person in the middle."
"There are always more desires than resources, something you celebrate because you want students to be proactive learners."	"I appreciate the energy of young members of the staff, but many are really very naïve about what I as a teacher can and can't do."
"Because I have a proven track record, they call on me to do more than I sometimes want to do."	"Some teachers nag, which I don't like, and yet I admire commitment."
	"As a woman teacher I always confront (have to deal with) the 'old boys' club.'"

Creative Leadership

Our discussion of contradictions, as the impetus for the interior tension that can lead to creativity rather than paralysis and depression, turns our attention to the age-old expression of wisdom: Know thyself.

The lifelong journey toward self-knowledge, a large part of which focuses on doing the psychological work to reconcile contradictions, can be healing. However, as Gloria Steinem (1992) notes in her provocative *Revolution From Within: A Book of Self-*

Esteem, the journey is also about "recovering the truest, most spontaneous, joyful, and creative core of ourselves" (p. 103). It is precisely this core that will help you as a teacher use your talents to help others identify and use their talents—our definition of creative leadership. It is this core that will foster your legacy. Steinem expresses this discovery of self in eloquent words: "Freeing an inner voice is a feeling of 'clicking in' when that self is recognized, valued, discovered, *esteemed*—as if we literally plug into an inner energy that is ours alone, yet connects us to everything else" (p. 26). Steinem adds, "Each of us has an inner child of the past living within us. Those who needed to build no walls have access to that child's creativity and spontaneity." She continues, "Those who had to leave this crucial core behind can tear down the walls, see what the child needed but didn't have, and begin to provide it now" (pp. 38-39).

In order to rediscover the sense of awe, wonder, and amazement you felt as a child, please write a paragraph or two in which you describe a particular childhood experience that stands out in your memory:

_____

_____

_____

_____

_____

Let us now see how others have responded to this exercise. A teacher in New Mexico said, "When I was a first grader I saw leaves on trees. They were so green and I wondered where they came from and why they danced in the wind." Another educator added, "When I saw my first caterpillar I let it crawl up and down my arm. I was six." A young teacher from Arizona described her engagement in the creative process:

> When I was 10 years old we got our first television set from the Firestone Store and we watched "I Love Lucy." I had my nose up to the screen, which taught my parents that I had eye trouble. I got glasses a week later. This made it possible for me to walk away from my mother in the grocery store for the first time. I could see!

Curiosity totally immerses a person in the excitement of learning. Time and place take a back seat to the excitement of the moment. "When I was little, there was a tremendous blizzard and snow covered the playground," a teacher said. She added, "I pretended I was in the South Pole and didn't hear the bell ring calling us back into school." Yo-Yo Ma, the brilliant young cellist, was asked about what he experienced during his 4½-hour concert, during which he played six Bach suites. He replied, "You are so into the music that you don't control it anymore. You are led by it." He concluded, "Bach takes you to a very quiet place within yourself, to the inner core, a place where you are calm and at peace" (Friedrich, 1991, p. 99).

Once we move out of early childhood, the battle between the forces of excitation and inhibition increases. One part of us urges us to get involved and take risks, while a second part tells us to stay back and play it safe. This is one of many contradictions that produce interior tension. The challenge is to use this interior tension to our advantage as teachers. Once we recognize that life is difficult but rewarding when we confront rather than run from problems, we sense our ability to make a difference in our own life and the lives of others. Life has meaning (Peck, 1978, p. 16).

We are at the place where we realize that awe, wonder, and amazement are natural by-products of exploration and we are challenged to ask, "How can I as a teacher structure my life so that I am engaged in creative processes that lead to awe, wonder, and amazement for myself and those I lead? How can I continue to experience the excitement of discovery that I felt as a child?" We may begin to answer the questions above by discussing two obstacles or pitfalls the creative teacher must avoid. *Excessive optimism,* assuming that things are naturally going to get better, is a way of denying or discounting real difficulties facing the teacher. It is also true that you can do your best to solve a problem or reconcile a dilemma and yet not reach your goal. Progress is not inevitable. A series of quotes from M. Scott Peck, psychiatrist and author of *The Road Less Traveled,* is helpful in relating to excessive optimism:

> Life is difficult . . . and once we truly see this truth, we transcend it.
>
> Discipline is the basic set of tools we require to solve life's problems.
>
> What makes life difficult is that the process of confronting and solving problems is a painful one. And since life poses an endless series of problems, life is always difficult and is full of pain as well as joy.
>
> Yet it is in this whole process of meeting and solving problems that life has its meaning. (1978, pp. 15-16)

It is precisely because of the downside of excessive optimism that leaders, such as Martin Luther King, Jr., made a distinction between optimism and hope. King argued that optimism can be used to leave people with the feeling that they have made a difference when they haven't done the work to make a difference (1968).

Pessimism is a second pitfall facing the creative teacher. Pessimism may be defined as the death of hope. Who wants to follow a leader who communicates no hope? The pessimist is self-indulgent and often attracts followers who also wallow in misery and victim-thinking. The leadership challenge was articulated by a producer who was concerned about his playwright's pessimism: "If you can't give the audience 'happy' (optimism) at least give them hope."

Now that we have discussed two major obstacles to the teacher as a creative leader, we can identify factors that facilitate creative leadership. These factors are actually characteristics of effective leaders, for it is effective leaders who create the conditions for others (such as our students) to choose to become creative leaders. The following checklist was constructed by teachers who observed effectiveness in their colleagues. Please use the checklist as you assess the leadership of a teacher you know. (You are invited to add items to the checklist.)

Characteristics of Teacher as an Effective Leader

_____ 1. Used applied intelligence (high-level common sense).

_____ 2. Was authoritative (had a sense of presence).

_____ 3. Did his/her homework (facts plus frameworks/ context).

_____ 4. An expert planner—left situation with concrete next steps in mind.

_____ 5. Sense of purpose (vision) stated clearly and referred to when appropriate. Clearly committed.

_____ 6. Listened well and spoke to persons at their level.

_____ 7. Fair.

_____ 8. Authentic or genuine (not phony).

_____ 9. Compassionate (not patronizing) and sensitive.

_____ 10. Not mean-spirited. Has a sense of humor.

_____ 11. Willing to take risks (make self vulnerable).

_____ 12. Trusts (able to "bracket" self and look at situation as if objective).

_____ 13. Good of the organization a primary consideration.

_____ 14. Able to build partnerships.

We have already presented the view that creative leadership is using one's talents to help others identify and use their talents. We have discovered that many teachers use their talents without having identified them as talents. We would like to have you fill out the following talent inventory in order to know better what talents you will share with those you teach and lead. There are three parts to this talent inventory: (1) describe one of your best days during the school year from the time you got up to the time you went to bed; (2) identify the talents you used during this day; and (3) name the people who helped you acquire and use these talents.

A Talent Inventory

Chronology of a Best School-Year Day	Talents I Used During the Day	People Who Helped Me Acquire and Use These Talents
7 a.m.: Got up		
_____		
_____		
_____		
_____		
_____		
_____		
_____		
_____		

In the following completed inventory you will see how one teacher's day began. Throughout the day she made a countless number of decisions that called on her creative abilities and talents.

A Talent Inventory		
Chronology of a Best School-Year Day	*Talents I Used During the Day*	*People Who Helped Me Acquire and Use These Talents*
7 a.m.: Got up	Responsible proactive person	Parents, teachers, mentors
Dressed in good clothes, groomed self	"	"
Greeted students with energetic smile	"	"
Opened well-organized lesson plans	Organizational skills	"
Began to teach using a special artifact form of "dig"	Interest in history and archaeology because of participation in a "dig" (initiative, attention to detail, etc.)	College professor/ mentor

In conclusion, we want to share with you our discovery that many people who had left teaching returned to it because of the creative opportunities for personal growth and the opportunity to help students develop their talents. Others have turned to teaching at a mid-career point because of the sameness of every-day activity in nonteaching occupations. The discovery of new ideas that can be shared with students is one of the main rewards in teaching—a legacy that would give anyone pride and satisfaction.

Yet at the same time, creativity is exacted at a price. As discussed in this section of the chapter, hard work has to be done in facing contradictions inherent in the teaching act itself. Cases or critical incidents in the following chapters give attention to conflicts, and therefore contradictions, facing the teacher as a decision maker.

PART II

Sources of Conflict in the School

In the preface to this book we discussed the advantages in using cases (critical incidents) as a way to stimulate discussion in staff development workshops, seminars, and classes for undergraduate and graduate students. We also noted the importance of teachers making a commitment to a particular course of action and providing the rationale for this commitment. One hallmark of the teacher as a professional is your ability to communicate to others what you have decided to do or have done and why.

In field-testing the cases in this book, we discovered that teachers want to be actively involved in staff development activities designed to improve their teaching. Stated another way, they do not want to be treated as empty vessels to be filled by lecturers. Case-based learning rests on the assumption that teachers as professionals can learn from each other when they enter into dialogue concerning the best response to a particular critical incident.

Once teachers get into the swing of reacting to cases, they discover that it is much like solving a puzzle. As one teacher remarked, "In many ways this is like video games that challenge us to constantly make decisions in order to come up with the best answers."

How Can We Teach and Learn From Cases in a Group Context?

We have developed a series of steps that we encourage you to use as a springboard that can be revised for your own purposes:

1. Assign a case or a limited number of cases to participants.

2. Ask participants to think about this assignment as one might think about writing a menu for a restaurant. List all possible or logically defensible responses.

   2.1. If the case is identified as a philosophical one, locate responses on the five-point continuum in the next section of this introduction.
   2.2. If the case is identified as a technical one, choose the best response from the alternatives and build a rationale for your choice.
   2.3. Compare and contrast your response to the authors' responses. (Revise your judgments only if you are convinced to do so.)

3. Discuss responses ("menus") in groups of three to five people, with one person acting as recorder. (Remember the ground rule is that everyone has the chance to be heard while others suspend judgment.)

   3.1. Work toward group consensus that can be defended in class by the recorder. (Minority responses are invited.)

There may be occasions when you have identified two responses that may be debated in a semiformal session by two groups who feel strongly that their position is correct. Once again, active involvement by participants is your key to successful staff development and class sessions.

The cases (critical incidents) in the remainder of the book call for responses of two kinds: (a) philosophical and (b) technical. Your philosophy of teaching consists of your basic assumptions as to what should be taught and how it should be taught. We have adopted a two camp philosophical framework, essentialist and progressive, in which your responses to cases will tend to fall. These camps have rich traditions in the history of American education.

We are well aware that there are many more philosophies of teaching, but we have chosen the essentialist and progressive camps in order to stimulate reflection, analysis, commitment, and discussion. It is our intent to help you construct a personal philosophy of teaching that will assist you in understanding and articulating particular decisions you make in the classroom and the school.

The five-point continuum we have used to display philosophical responses to cases consists of extreme essentialist and progressive positions with three points in between:

Essentialist				*Progressive*
Strongly agree	Mildly agree	Neutral	Mildly agree	Strongly agree

We suggest that you place your preferred response to a philosophical case on this continuum. You may then discuss agreement and disagreement in a small and/or large group setting.

Cases at the end of each chapter are more technical in nature. You are asked to identify possible responses from which you choose a preferred response and provide a rationale for it. Then, compare and contrast your response and rationale to the authors' preferred response and rationale.

Much if not most of your teaching day will probably be free of conflict. However, squarely facing and working through critical incidents (cases) may lead to your greatest growth as a teacher. It will be the key to your success as a teacher.

Two Philosophical Camps: A Framework for Teachers

We will devote the remainder of this introduction to a discussion of essentialism and progressivism as they relate to teaching practices. You may then apply this background knowledge to decisions you make in responding to particular cases.

Essentialism

Essentialism in America has been called the educational philosophy of the conservative because its advocates give primary attention to conserving what they think is the best of the past. They believe that the school's main purpose is to transfer to youth the accumulated knowledge and traditions of the human race. The kind of knowledge they wish to pass on is traditional knowledge. It is tried and tested knowledge that has stood the test of time. For this reason this knowledge is often referred to as our "cultural heritage" (Morris, 1961). It is not the most recent knowledge that is taken from today's headlines. It is not even necessarily the "relevant" knowledge that students seem to always want.

Essentialists reject as being of little or no value the knowledge reflected in such course titles as:

"The Sociology of Hunger"
"Teenage Fiction"
"The Sociology of Alternative Life-Styles"
"African-American History"
"The History of Feminism in America"
"Literature of the Occult"

Such popular "mini-courses" have been commonplace in many of America's secondary schools. Essentialists think that such courses do not deserve equal academic credit with such subjects as algebra and ancient history. They do not contain essential knowledge passed on by scholars throughout the ages. Furthermore, is a question from any such course ever likely to turn up on a standardized achievement test or the Scholastic Aptitude Test? No, they say. Therefore, why encourage students to study such pap?

What do essentialists think schooling should be? Essentialists believe in education that stresses the fundamentals. Modern essentialists favor going "back to the basics" of the traditional curriculum as a course of study. These basics include the skills of reading, writing, and arithmetic—hence, English and mathematics. The basics also include a fundamental knowledge of history, science, and foreign language. These five subjects must be taught to each student, regardless of abilities or interests, every year, particularly in the secondary school (Morris, 1961).

Essentialists are opposed to what they see as the "permissiveness" and "anti-intellectualism" of progressivism in our schools. Progressives are their ideological enemies. Essentialists claim that progressives are premature in trying to teach students to think and solve problems before they have first acquired a body of reliable knowledge as a subject matter base. In other words, essentialists feel that you cannot think in terms of a vacuum. They believe that only "basic content" can give students a sense of historical perspective and tradition (Morris, 1961).

In summary, then, the essence of essentialism is that all American children should have to learn the fundamental arts of reading, writing, spelling, measurement and computation, and history in the elementary schools. These should be the essentials for *all* American students. Essentialists favor studying subjects as separate disciplines—not as some hodgepodge called "language arts," "social studies," or "humanities." Essentialists believe that such combination subjects lack real substance or integrity. On the other hand, if subjects are studied as separate disciplines, students can understand the viewpoint, structure, and method of each discipline (Morris, 1961).

The essentialist further believes that the student should master the subject matter of a given grade level before he or she is promoted to the next grade level. In other words, the essentialist believes in retaining failing students in the same grade rather than giving them "social promotions" to keep them with students of the same chronological age.

Finally, essentialists believe that students should master "the essentials" before they are allowed to study other less essential material that is possibly more interesting to them.

What is the essentialist position with regard to particular educational issues?

Ability grouping keeps the gifted student from being cheated. Essentialists claim that in a class of all ability levels (heterogeneous) the teacher aims the level of instruction at the mediocre and slow pupil. To counteract this, many essentialists would like to have a separate academic track for the gifted, such as college preparatory, within a heterogeneous school, thus separating them from general, commercial, and special education students. Barring this, essentialists would favor homogeneous grouping within a single track (curriculum) in order to segregate the gifted students. This means segregating students into ability sections. This is purportedly done to best accommodate individual student differences. Typically, this is done on the basis of achievement test scores, I.Q. (perhaps with a cutoff score of, for example, 120 for the gifted), grades, and teacher recommendations. Historically, such ability grouping has been done in English, math, science, and languages. Generally, there has been no ability grouping in the "less academic" subjects of physical education, art, and the social studies (Morris, 1961).

Seating arrangements, according to the essentialist position, should usually be done traditionally. Rows of desks discourage pupil interaction with one another. We should focus attention on the teacher as an instructor. Teachers introduce subject matter and serve as a screen for student responses. Because students do not have the knowledge base essential to informed dialogue, such dialogue is discounted by many essentialists as a "pooling of ignorance." Students seated in rows set the tone for the social and emotional climate necessary in order to learn objective knowledge (Morris, 1961).

Subject matter centers on the essential knowledge of the past. "I teach English" is how the teacher generally describes his occupational purpose, whereas the progressive is more likely to focus his comments on children or young people. Because of their subject-centered approach, essentialists tend to become upset about interruptions to the class routine. Taking class time for intercom announcements, special assemblies, pep rallies, athletic events and trips, club periods, and collecting money really irritates the essentialist. Such activities distract teachers and students from "covering the material" (Morris, 1961).

Teaching methods and materials advocated by the essentialist are based on the assumption that the teacher is the most important and knowledgeable person in the classroom. The lecture method is generally preferred. This is basically "teaching by telling," or the expository method. When done well, the lecture method can be used to describe, define, explain, analyze, inquire, provoke, arouse, and excite (Morris, 1961).

Textbooks and the chalkboard are relied on heavily by the essentialist teacher. Books are an avenue to the past and give the student summations of articulate people who have established themselves as subject-matter experts (Morris, 1961).

Classroom discipline is an essentialist first step for student learning. Two key questions are addressed by the essentialist: (a) How should the student be controlled? (b) How should the student be taught to control himself or herself? The essentialist believes that a student is taught how to control himself or herself by being controlled by the teacher—repeatedly. In other words, self-discipline comes from being disciplined. Students learn restraint by being restrained.

Schools function *in loco parentis* (in place of the parents) by invoking rules and penalties (Morris, 1961). Students' opinions with regard to such rules and penalties are irrelevant. Penalties may include:

Verbal rebukes
Isolation from others in class
Denial of privileges

Trip to the principal's office

Keeping in after school

Corporal punishment (in some states and school systems).

An important point to remember is that an essentialist generally doesn't give primary attention to discipline as a learning experience, but rather sees discipline as a means used by the teacher to facilitate learning in the classroom (Morris, 1961).

Testing and evaluation play an important role in the essentialist position. Generally, the essentialist is concerned about the intellectual growth of students—not their social, emotional, or physical development. (These are the responsibility of other social agencies, such as the family.) Objective paper and pencil achievement tests are valuable because right or wrong answers are obvious. Essay exams are useful to see if students have learned essential ideas from the text and teacher (Morris, 1961).

Essentialists talk a great deal about "maintaining standards," by which is meant teacher-decided criteria of academic achievement. The essentialist does not generally take into account individual and class differences in abilities when giving out grades. Grading on the curve is often done in an attempt to quantify everything and render into mathematical statistics the comparative achievements of students. This practice presupposes a "normal distribution" of academic aptitude in each class of students (Morris, 1961). Essentialists use grades to certify to other constituencies, such as parents, subsequent teachers, colleges, other schools, and potential employers, how well a student has mastered the subject matter taught.

Progressivism

Progressivism is the educational philosophy of the "nontraditionalist." It is an experience-based, practical system of thinking. Because of its experience-centered core, progressivism holds that reality is different for each of us. That is, none of us have an identical set of life experiences. Therefore, our viewpoints (or perceptions and values) are bound to differ (Morris, 1961). With regard to truth, the progressive's view is that ideas should be tested for their utility or usefulness. If an idea works out in practice, then we can accept it, use it, and call it *truth*. If an idea does not work, the pragmatist scraps the idea, learns from his experience, and tries something new. To a progressive, then, *truth* is what works. (It is easy to see how this philosophy was appealing to the ever-expanding frontier mentality of early Americans.) A corollary of this statement is: "Truth is not absolute, but relative to the perceiver and the circumstances in a given time and place" (Morris, 1961, pp. 368-369). According to this view, what works for me in a given situation is truth for me. But it may not be truth for you. Why not? Because your circumstances might be different, and all truth is relative to its surrounding circumstances of place and time. For example, would it have been a truth in 1955 to say "man can walk on the moon"? No. Would this have been truth in 1969? Yes. This year, would it be a truth that man can create an exact replica of a living human being through cloning? No. What will be the answer to this question in the year 2010? One simply does not know.

The progressive believes that ethically, whether something is "good" or "bad" is determined by the public test. In other words, if we try something out, it will prove to be either good or bad in terms of its consequences for the welfare of ourselves and/or others (Morris, 1961).

Aesthetically, that which is beautiful is whatever squares with the public taste. For example, if most people think that a piece of sculpture is a beautiful artifact, then it is, by definition, beautiful.

The leading spokesman for progressivism was the philosopher John Dewey. In his writings, Dewey emphasized a generalized problem-solving procedure that is similar to the scientific method. The problem-solving procedure is a means by which we find out what works in a given situation. Dewey saw this problem-solving procedure as one and the same with the process of education. He believed that the procedure could be effectively applied to problems in the physical or biological sciences, or to a social or personal problem.

Most progressives are committed to change and progress in our society. They feel that change is inevitable and that we should therefore learn how to manage it so that mankind can be "in the saddle," directing change rather than having "events in the saddle," leading us to some unknown destination. Most progressives feel that the process of inquiry or problem solving is the proper tool for managing change. Thus, such a process has utility for us. In this way, our society can constantly renew, sustain, and propagate itself. Progress, then, is simply a by-product.

In essence, progressive education is "learning through living." In living, we are constantly confronted with change—the only constant. Young people must learn to manage change in the experiences of everyday living. Progressives advocate no prescribed curriculum and therefore no fixed sequence of subject matter (Morris, 1961).

What subject matter is dealt with in a progressive's classroom? It is subject matter that is relevant to the solution of a problem that interests the individual learner. Progressives contend that if a student learns that which interests him or her, it will be "real" learning and not forced learning, which merely leads to memorization and regurgitation (Morris, 1961). Progressives place a heavy emphasis on students working together in the context of a group. This is logical because several students might be interested in inquiring into the same "problem." Progressives tend to favor group work as an educational end in itself because it enables students to be socialized to one another. In other words, students learn how to work with persons of a different race, sex, age, ethnic background, religion, and the like. This experience should serve them well as adults, when they must frequently work with others on the job, in religious settings, on community boards, and the like (Morris, 1961).

Because the world is constantly changing, progressives think that it is futile to try to teach a given body of knowledge in the hope that it will serve the student well in his or her life for 10 to 20 years. Progressives point out that in certain fields, such as biology and astronomy, knowledge is changing so fast that any textbook is outdated in some very important ways as soon as it appears on the market. To a progressive, the process of learning is far more important than any content or subject matter learned. The process endures, but most content is quickly outdated (Morris, 1961).

In a progressive's classroom, there is a desire to deal with open, controversial questions and problems. They accuse essentialists of treating closed, pedantic questions with safe, right answers (Morris, 1961).

Finally, a very important tenet of progressive ideology is that the teacher is a fellow-learner along with the student. Progressives view the teacher's proper role as that of a stimulator of interests, a helper, and a resource person. The idea of forcing a student to learn is foreign to the progressive. The progressive encourages rather than requires. The language of understanding rather than control is used by the progressive (Morris, 1961).

Probably no single issue philosophically divides progressive and essentialist educators as much as the issue of homogeneous ability grouping. Progressives are opposed to any type of ability grouping or any type of segregation of students of the same chronological age, whether it is done on the basis of sex, race, social class, or academic performance. Progressives contend that students need to have as much exposure as possible to all kinds of people. They feel that ability grouping destroys the socializing power of the school and yields "undemocratic" by-products, such as entitlement, snobbery, and condescension. Progressives argue that heterogeneous grouping assures each student of an equal chance to an education. Moreover, they contend that students of all types can learn much from each other. Progressives, therefore, support the concept of mainstreaming all exceptional children—for example, gifted and talented, learning disabled, retarded, emotionally or physically handicapped (Morris, 1961).

Classroom seating is an important issue to many progressive educators. Because of the influence of progressive educators, we now have movable furniture in most of our school classrooms instead of desks bolted to the floor. Individual desks, or tables and chairs, or temporary seating on carpeted areas enable the teacher to have infinite seating patterns for different tasks in the classroom. Movable furniture facilitates interaction between students in a classroom, and progressives highly value such interaction because they believe that students can learn much from one another (Morris, 1961).

Preferred teaching methods center on the belief that the teacher is first and foremost a teacher of children or young people, rather than a teacher of a particular subject. Consequently, the progressive uses little or no lecture, recitation, and demonstration. As fellow inquirers, the progressive favors the problem-solving method or the project method. In carrying out a project, students have to use or apply much present knowledge. In addition, they uncover considerable new knowledge through their research. Progressives feel that it is in the use of knowledge that students really learn in a meaningful way. A living awareness of subject matter is superior to memorizing subject matter prescribed by some authority and giving it back on a test (Morris, 1961).

If textbooks are used, they are used in a selective way. (After all, what text author ever met *your* class? You know your students and their interests best.) The progressive also selectively uses a variety of materials on the basis of their utility in assembling information concerning a problem under investigation (Morris, 1961).

Preferred subject matter is a subject of concern only in that such subject matter fits an interdisciplinary curriculum. That is, no one discipline has a "corner on the market" with regard to solving a problem. The teacher is an artist and scientist who uses his or her expertise to guide students in their interdisciplinary pursuits (Morris, 1961).

Discipline, according to the progressive, is best when it is self-discipline. In the progressive's view, self-discipline is learned gradually when the child is given opportunities to control self, while being prompted by a set of rules that he has had the opportunity to help formulate. Positive reinforcement is a key tool used by the progressive teacher (Morris, 1961).

Testing and evaluation, according to the progressive, should be primarily qualitative rather than quantitative. Student portfolios present the teacher with many and diverse examples of a student's work over a period of time. The progressive is also interested in sociometric evaluation procedures that focus on progress in group-interaction skills. Self-evaluation is another important tool used by progressive educators (Morris, 1961). Their evaluation is process-oriented; hence, criterion- or norm-referenced tests of achievement have little weight in a progressive's evaluation procedures.

Progressives point to research that demonstrates that grade-level retention is counterproductive. Even though they are accused of "social promotions," progressives point out the damage done when students are stigmatized by failure. Furthermore, progressives argue that a student's transcript gives a future employer a qualitative picture of progress, without resorting to further labeling a student as a failure.

In conclusion, you, the leader, should find that your responses to many of the cases will tend to place you in either the essentialist or the progressive camp. By engaging in this process, you will not only know where you stand but you will also be better able to understand the philosophical or ideological positions of your fellow students or colleagues.

Finally, as stated before, not all cases have responses that may be classified as essentialist or progressive. Some cases are more technical and are not grounded in a philosophical position. We have placed cases that accommodate philosophical responses in the beginning of each chapter.

3 STUDENT–TEACHER CONFLICT

Few books in the history of education have had the impact of Yale psychologist Seymour Sarason's *The Culture of the School and the Problem of Change.* It was originally published in 1971, and its second edition's continuing popularity is attested to by the number of printings it has undergone. Sarason's emphasis on the culture of the school helps us see that school settings are much more than an assemblage of individuals in a physical structure. Every school has its own *Zeitgeist* or "what's in the air," which is based on existing behavioral and programmatic regularities directed toward intended outcomes (Sarason, 1971). In Chapter 3, "University and School Cultures," Sarason describes these two cultures as if he is observing them from a space platform (Sarason, 1971). Although the two cultures appear to be as different as apples and oranges, they are in fact comparable in many respects. For example, they are hierarchically and elaborately organized so that change is slow, and "deviant" proposals tend to be screened out (Sarason, 1971). Sarason's conclusions in this regard are fascinating to observe for the simple reason that when

43

college students in teacher preparation programs move into schools as teachers, they quickly adjust to hierarchical regularities. They are simply at a higher place in the hierarchy than they were as college or university students. This was reflected in a beginning teacher's comment that finally he had reached a position where he could do to students what had been done to him.

The Teacher as Authority Figure

The difficulty with the beginning teacher's easy adjustment to school culture hierarchy is that our global society outside the school and university has, in recent years, challenged the very nature of traditional bureaucratic power arrangements. Specifically, positional authority as a source of power no longer has the acceptance it once had, compared to emerging sources of power, such as expertise, charisma, and the ability to give succor. This reality was brought home to us by a 40-year-old teacher whose mother still lives in the mountains of North Carolina. He told the following story:

> Our family doctor in the mountains told my mother that she must immediately prepare herself psychologically and physically for surgery in order to amputate a leg ravaged by sugar diabetes. The general practitioner added that her other leg would also have to be amputated in due time. Our family had always trusted the professional judgment (positional authority) of this physician, and my mother prepared herself for surgery. It just didn't seem right to me, however, and so I talked her into going with me to Winston-Salem, North Carolina, a 2-hour drive from our home that we almost never made when we were children. A specialist at Wake Forest's Bowman Gray School of Medicine said that amputation was not necessary, given newly found ways of treating diabetes. My mother has been walking around well for 15 years on legs our family doctor was preparing to remove.

Teachers are facing the same challenges to positional authority that the mountain doctor in this story faced. They have some students who know more about computers than they do, and they have other students who, because of television, family conversations and travel, know more about world events than they as teachers know. "I'm right (know more) because of my position of authority as a teacher" simply won't be accepted as it once was. Teachers who know what they don't know and are committed to doing something to learn what they don't know meet the challenging realities of the new global society. They thrive on the discovery of new ideas, many of which they learn from their students. Teachers who do not think they are up to this challenge retreat to traditional authority mechanisms and are isolated by their students from their own classrooms. A covenant is often formed, whereby students and teachers agree to spend the year together with nothing important happening for either party. (The student is, however, ensured of a good grade if he or she "plays along.") In effect, both parties have dropped out of the learning process. When the teacher and students are actively involved in the learning process, they formally or informally agree on how they will help each other use human and non-human resources to reach commonly agreed-on goals. In the process, they become so focused on tasks to be performed that discipline and classroom management are rarely a problem. We recently witnessed this in a middle school learning laboratory center. Seventy-five computers were being used. Collaborative learning was the norm as students integrated learning from science, math, language arts, and social studies. The key to this success was teamwork among the technology specialist and two middle school teachers.

The Matter of Discipline

Teachers who are genuinely curious and have a passion for learning have taken the first step in a preventive discipline program. This passion for learning will create energy that will communicate to students: "I want to be with you." Effective teachers' commitment to preventive discipline may explain in part why recent Gallup polls indicate distance between parents' and teachers' views of how important a problem discipline is. The general public ranked discipline among the three biggest problems schools face in their communities, among six national goals and among two highest factors they consider in the selection of a school for their child, and first among suggestions for helping low-income and racial or ethnic minorities succeed in school. Teachers, on the other hand, perceive discipline problems as less serious than parents' lack of interest and support, lack of proper financial support, and students' lack of interest and truancy (Elam, Rose, & Gallup, 1991, 1992).

There is hope in that support by parents and teachers for professional autonomy, often in the name of site-based management, is indicated in recent polls (Elam et al., 1991, 1992). However, there is contradictory evidence in such polls in that parents want accountability measures, such as a national report card that compares schools and more emphasis on tests, that bureaucratize school culture (Elam et al., 1991, 1992).

What is clear from national surveys or polls and research about the culture of the school is that students are rarely asked their opinion as to what schools should and can be. That is, they are "done unto" rather than with, which is to say that they are not involved in the covenant formation process that could create meaning in their lives and the lives of their teachers and school administrators. As a result, teachers act out a contradiction: They know what drives them forward in the learning process, but "their inability to see or assume some kinds of identity between their pupils and themselves leads them unwittingly to create those conditions that they would personally find boring" (Sarason, 1971, p. 222). In short, students are seldom asked to participate in forming covenants with teachers for learning and, as a result, don't "own" the learning process itself.

The theme and thesis of this section of the introduction is that meaningful teacher-student covenants preclude discipline problems for the most part.

Conclusion

Today's students face a number of societal problems that were not faced by earlier generations: a divorce epidemic, drugs, violence, unclear moral standards, teenage pregnancy, and pressure to spend money that benefits an adult economy. It has been argued in this introduction that prospective and present teachers need to understand our new global society in order to connect with today's students. This understanding will be the basis for specific details in covenants formed between adult educators and students. The cases that follow demonstrate the challenge we face in creating and maintaining covenants that bring meaning to the lives of educators and students.

Case 3.1: Student Wants Grade for Effort

You, the teacher, have just handed back papers to your students. One student comes up to you and asks why students who spent less time on their papers got higher grades. The student adds, "I spent 5 hours on my paper and I think that effort should be considered when you assign grades."

What is your response?

(extreme response) Progressive	neutral	(extreme response) Essentialist
This case illustrates the downside of a highly competitive society in which results are more important than process. Emphasis on product and accountability discount process, including effort. Assure the student that effort does count in the long run. Also make it clear that there is no truly "objective" system of evaluation, and you will consider effort in the assignment of final grades. Circumstances must be considered in the evaluation of a student's work.		This case has a clear answer. One either learns essential knowledge or one does not. There are predetermined standards against which the quality of an individual's work is assessed. It is a reality that society rewards results (the product) rather than the process (including effort). It is your responsibility as a teacher to make this lesson in life clear to the student. It is not appropriate to evaluate one student's effort vis-à-vis another student's effort. Once again, evaluation is done with respect to predetermined standards.

Case 3.2: Your Reaction to a Situation in Which Your Authority as a Teacher Is Being Challenged by a Student

You are teaching a history lesson and your training is in economics. You find that there is one exceptionally bright student in the class who seems to know more history than you do and uses every opportunity to show this knowledge at your expense. The other students are aware that this particular student may, in fact, know more than you, and this is beginning to affect your authority in the classroom because the student answers questions that you cannot. The student begins to cause you a good deal of anxiety.

How will you handle this situation?

(extreme response) Progressive	neutral	*(extreme response)* Essentialist
This case proves the "correctness" of the progressive's position. The learning process is paramount. The appearance of always being "right" and in charge is a heavy burden for the essentialist to bear. Use any resources available to get the job done. Draw on the expertise of the bright student—a good leadership lesson for the students. If you continue to be assigned the history class, find ways to learn more about the subject.		This case is a dilemma for the essentialist: The authority of the teacher is essential for a well-managed classroom, yet the teacher doesn't have the essential knowledge in history to teach well at the moment. You will simply have to make do at the present time, but you must do whatever is necessary as soon as possible to gain the essential knowledge. Or, you may decide it is best to avoid recognizing the bright student in order to reinforce your authority.

Case 3.3: Bright Student Takes Over the Class

A student in your algebra class participated in a Talent Search Program over the summer. She took an intensive 3-week course in Algebra I. Unfortunately, she has no choice but to repeat the course during the regular school year. Since she has had the advantage of exposure to more complex skills in algebra, she tries to "teach" the class a "better way" every time you introduce a new topic. The class will eventually learn these skills, but they are not ready for them yet.

What will you do?

(extreme response) *Progressive*	*neutral*	(extreme response) *Essentialist*
Explain to the student that it is necessary for the class to learn the simpler processes first. Whenever possible, call on her to help with peer tutoring. Try to understand the student's frustration and challenge her with special assignments.		Challenge the student to further enhance her knowledge base in any way possible, but make it clear to her that you are the teacher and your position of authority must be maintained so as to not confuse her peers.

Case 3.4: Student Accuses You of Racism

At the beginning of the school year, a student in a pre-algebra class is made aware (through her classmates) that you are allowing others to move into algebra. She also wants to do this. She is an average student and you do not feel that she will be successful.

After giving her your reasons for not recommending the move, the student accuses you of racism.

How will you respond?

(extreme response) Progressive	neutral	*(extreme response)* Essentialist
Allow her to move to Algebra I and see how well she does. Be sure she has every advantage. Sorting mechanisms, such as grades, are often arbitrary. Although you don't appreciate being called a racist, respect the student's "spunk," an essential life skill.		You are the subject matter expert and are in a better position than anyone to judge her readiness for advancing to Algebra I. Let your decision stand.

Case 3.5: Student Approaches You for Advice on Sex

A student in your high school math class approaches you after class and asks if she can talk to you after school when it is convenient. You assume that the conversation will involve a college recommendation, a question about a math problem, or another school-related matter, so you immediately tell her to drop by after seventh period.

When the student arrives, she proceeds to tell you that she respects your opinions and values and would like to discuss an important decision with you. The student shocks you by asking you for advice about having sex with her boyfriend. She says she does not feel comfortable talking with her family and she needs some guidance about making this decision.

What will you do?

(extreme response) Progressive	neutral	(extreme response) Essentialist
Your care for the student and the importance of this decision should be communicated. Also, thank the student for her confidence in you as a teacher. Encourage the student, if she wishes to talk, to explore options and the responsibilities for each decision she may make. Serve as a "broker" who helps her get more professional help, such as a good counselor from your school. Recognize, however, that you are in a sensitive position.		Tell the student that sex is a very personal matter that should be discussed with her family and experts who have the knowledge that is required to advise her in a professional way. Do not get involved beyond that because your primary role is to impart subject matter.

Case 3.6: Student Abused Because of Poor Grades

You arrive at school one morning and are surprised by one of your students and his father. You are very polite to the child and the parent and invite them into the classroom. The father remarks, "You won't have another problem with my son making D's. We got that straightened out, didn't we, boy?"

As the father leaves, you remember that report cards were passed out yesterday, and Roger made a D in math. As you talk to Roger, you uncover an explanation for the angry comment, and he tells you he received a beating for this bad grade. You tell Roger to sit down. He says he can't because it is too painful. You inquire about the regularity of the beatings and discover that they only occur when Roger gets a bad grade.

How will you react to this unfortunate incident?

(extreme response) *Progressive*	*neutral*	*(extreme response)* *Essentialist*
Report this matter to the principal, who must be informed officially about this beating. Talk to Roger about the extent of his abuse, so you will understand how his home situation affects his school performance. The school must get involved in cases like this to provide a safe refuge for students.		Report this matter to the principal for official/legal reasons. Consult those with expertise and knowledge on these matters, but don't cross the line so that Roger thinks you are claiming expertise and special knowledge on these matters. Agencies outside of the school should deal with these matters so that essential academic functions aren't distracted.

Case 3.7: Classmates Mistreat Student

You are the teacher of a class of 24 third graders. You notice that they all pick on one boy, Joey. No one will sit with him at lunch, talk with him at break, or play with him at recess.

Joey has a poor home life, and you can see that he is obviously hurt by the class's treatment of him.

What will you do?

(extreme response) *Progressive*	*neutral*	(extreme response) *Essentialist*
Make a special effort to spend some personal time with Joey each day. Discuss in class the importance of treating others as you would like to be treated. (Do not single Joey out.) Discuss this situation with the guidance counselor and solicit her professional advice. On occasion, pair Joey with a popular child on the playground, and so on.		As the authority in the classroom, you set rules, including rules that deal with this situation. Admonish the offending students. Then, talk to the guidance counselor—perhaps with Joey making weekly visits. The counselor is the expert on such matters. A situation like this can affect the academic achievement of all children.

Case 3.8: Sarcastic Student Interrupts Class

You are at your best while teaching a particular lesson when a student who is sitting at the rear of the room starts making sarcastic comments, which the rest of the students find very amusing and entertaining. The student speaks out in class, interrupting your lesson at will.

What will you do?

(extreme response) Progressive	neutral	*(extreme response)* Essentialist
Self-control is one aim of education. It is important for the teacher to understand the cause or causes of misbehavior, after which both the student and teacher will learn what is necessary for the student to behave in more acceptable ways. Therefore, have a private talk with the offending student. It is important to recognize that we all learn from our mistakes.		Classroom discipline is an essential first step for student learning. Students must be controlled so that they learn to control themselves. A number of penalties may be invoked to teach the sarcastic student to behave: verbal rebukes, isolation from others, denial of privileges, a trip to the principal's office, or keeping him after school.

Case 3.9: A Student Cheats on an Exam

During an important test, you observe a student cheating. It was done through reference to notes. The student does not realize you have spotted him, nor do other students seem to realize what has been happening.

What will you do?

(extreme response) Progressive	neutral	(extreme response) Essentialist
A progressive is concerned with students' learning from their mistakes. Say nothing at the time, but tell the student to report to you during his study hall or after school that day. At the appointed time, make it clear to the student that you are concerned about possible testing irregularities and insist that he retake the same test right there under carefully monitored conditions. Grade both tests and have the student explain any discrepancy in grades to you and perhaps his parents.		An essentialist must maintain high academic standards, and cheating is never tolerated. Take the test paper and notes on the spot. To make the situation an example to others, inform the student aloud that he will receive a zero on the test.

Case 3.10: Student Swears in Class

Shortly before class is to be dismissed, a once-retained, nice, but very socially, psychologically, and academically immature student uses language identified as swearing by classmates and you. All eyes turn toward you.

What will you do?

(extreme response) Progressive	neutral	*(extreme response)* Essentialist
This is certainly not a major offense. However, the classroom is a "miniature society" and as such is a good place to practice civilities that will stand students well when they graduate. Take the student aside and point out that swearing is unacceptable in class. Tell him that you will help him monitor his behavior to not swear. Ask him how he could have made the same point, using socially acceptable language. This makes the encounter a learning experience.		Your authority as a teacher must be clear to students at all times. The student must be disciplined promptly so that he doesn't swear again. Staying after school may be appropriate. Swearing is one of many acts that can detract from an academic tone in class.

Case 3.11: Student Passes Notes

You are conducting a class and you observe a student passing notes. How will you handle this situation?

(extreme response) Progressive	neutral	(extreme response) Essentialist
Behavior like this must be understood in terms of context. That is, the forming of a class "constitution" is the first step the teacher should attend to at the start of the year. Students and teacher must decide what behaviors are acceptable and what behaviors are unacceptable. It is the process of forming the "constitution" that sets the stage for the remainder of the year. Although a minor infraction, note passing can be distracting, and the class should help you bring to the student's attention that this behavior is unacceptable.		Note passing is unacceptable, and your established authority should be used to stop it. It gets in the way of learning. A first-time warning should be followed by more drastic action, such as seizing the note or lowering the grade.

Case 3.12: Reaching a Student With Recent Problems

A student who was doing good work has recently had a number of problems. You assigned a paper, which counts for one third of the grade that term. On the day the papers were due, the student informed you that the paper was lost on the way to school. You assigned a book review. All information needed was explained, including the due date. Adequate time was allowed. All but this one student turned in the report when requested. Her report was turned in late. After handing back an important test, this student came up to you and said she was tired and performed poorly because her parents were fighting all night.

What will you do?

(extreme response) *Progressive*	*neutral*	(extreme response) *Essentialist*
This student's personal life has obviously changed in recent months, thus adversely influencing work at school. The only information you have at the moment is that the student's parents have been fighting. What you do know is that someone in the school setting must intervene to get more information, after which the school and you can help the student get back on track. Talk to and work with a counselor trusted by the student. Be alert as you make a special effort to reach this at-risk student.		This student's academic future is in trouble unless something is done. Primary responsibility for the student's personal life is in the hands of her parents. Contact the parents, assure them of your interest in their child's academic future, and share the student's recent history of problems. Do not inquire about the student's home situation, because you are not a counselor.

Case 3.13: Students Misbehave at an Assembly

Faculty members are not required to sit with their students at school assemblies. The school does not have an auditorium as yet, and assemblies are held in the gymnasium.

The city's symphony orchestra is playing at this assembly. Four or five young men, not in your classes, are sitting at the top of the bleachers and deliberately making noise; for example, they are dropping books to the floor from the top of the bleachers.

There are no teachers near the disruptive students. In fact, there are almost no teachers at the assembly.

What will you do? Choose the best of the following responses:

1. Talk to the superintendent of schools at your first opportunity—perhaps in an informal setting, rather than making an appointment. Spell out your concern about student behavior in the school in general and assemblies in particular, as well as lack of teacher participation at assemblies.
2. Talk to the principal of the school and voice your strong feelings about student behavior at assemblies and lack of teacher participation at these gatherings.
3. Do nothing. Just ride it out.
4. Take this matter to the faculty advisory council. If the council is ineffective, give leadership to bring life to it.
5. Move to the scene of the disturbance during the assembly and discipline the students on the spot.

Case 3.13: Rationales for the Alternative Responses

1. The school is obviously in disarray and it is clear that the principal is ineffective. Only a few teachers have even shown up for the assemblies. Drastic measures are called for, and this means going over the head of the principal. The advantage of talking to the superintendent in an informal setting is that there is no formal record of your meeting with the superintendent, and therefore there is no formal need for the superintendent to let your principal know that you have talked to the superintendent about

the matter. Information is power, and this information, when given to the proper person, can bring about needed change. This response may be needed, but it is probably best not to start with it. If other measures fail, use this response. Search for a better initial response.

2. The principal is officially responsible for all matters in the school, including discipline at assemblies. Talking to the principal is straightforward and honest, and you won't be criticized as a tattletale for going over the principal's head to the superintendent and/or gossiping around the school. However, matters are obviously out of hand with regard to discipline at assemblies, and the principal's leadership is likely ineffective. Therefore, search for a better response.

3. This is the best way to catch no flack from anyone. Retreat to your classroom whenever possible, and perhaps don't go to assemblies yourself in the future. The problem with this response is that it leads to a kind of cynicism that is deadly among faculty and a poor example for students. You take care of yourself and those in your "kingdom" (the classroom) but don't assume responsibility for total school matters.

4. This is the best choice for the moment. You and your colleagues must come together and take action, even though it is difficult to do with an ineffective principal. (You end up doing the principal's work as faculty members.) The discipline problem in assemblies (and probably elsewhere in the school) must be thoroughly discussed, and a plan of action must be implemented.

5. At first look this seems like a good response. However, you must remember that this is a gymnasium with bleachers, and students are dropping books from the top of the bleachers. There is no way for you to make your way to them without being obtrusive and calling a good deal of attention to yourself. If you were the principal, you could stop the assembly between orchestra selections to get order, but the principal, who is probably in the gymnasium, has not given any leadership in this situation. Therefore, you should probably reject this option and search for a better one.

Case 3.14: Student Is Caught Smoking in a Restroom

Your school has rigidly enforced a no-smoking rule on school grounds. You excuse yourself at the lunch table and leave your colleagues to enter the restroom, which is used by faculty and students alike. A student is at the sink with a lighted cigarette.

What will you do? Choose the best response from the following alternatives:

1. Tell the student to put it out—and you are glad that you didn't see what had happened.
2. Inform the student of the school rule and say that if you catch the student again, you will report the student to the office.
3. Inform the student that you will report the infraction to the principal or assistant principal.
4. Say nothing and do nothing about the incident.

Case 3.14: Rationales for the Alternative Responses

1. This approach has the advantage of letting the student know you saw what was happening, but chose not to deal with it this time. The student will know that you aren't rigid. However, this is a potentially bad option because others may observe you doing nothing and/or the student will tell others that you didn't enforce the no-smoking rule. Find a better response.
2. The student will know that you aren't rigid and will give the student a second chance. However, once again the student and friends will know that you didn't enforce the school rule. Seek a better response.
3. This is probably the best response. The school rule has been in effect for some time, and all expect you to enforce it. By enforcing this rule you will have a cleaner building and cleaner air as well.
4. This takes fewer resources than any other responses. However, you will be known as a teacher who doesn't take leadership responsibility. Search for a better response.

Case 3.15: Your Reaction to Romantic Involvement of One of Your Students

You are an excellent teacher and, over a period of weeks, you notice that a student has a crush on you and insists on lingering after class each day and running into you as you leave school. The situation grows more serious, to the point of embarrassment. The student constantly offers to help you collect papers, hand out assignments, and run general errands. You begin to sense resentment in the class for what appears to be your "favored" treatment of the student.

How will you deal with this situation? Choose the best alternative from the following responses:

1. Pay less attention to the student's offers of help for a few days. Avoid the student in the halls and after school. Choose a number of students to help you around the classroom.
2. Talk to the student privately about the matter.
3. Talk to the principal about this matter to "cover your bases."

Case 3.15: Rationales for the Alternative Responses

1. This is probably the best response. You need to deal with this matter by distancing yourself from the student, but not excluding the student from your teaching behavior. By deliberately involving all students, you will demonstrate that you don't play favorites.
2. This approach deals with the problem directly so that the student knows where you stand. The difficulty with this option is that this is a very sensitive matter that can be misread and misunderstood easily. Try another option.
3. This is the best way to cover yourself immediately in a bureaucratic way. It is a good second choice and may become necessary if the problem persists. Try another response at this time.

Case 3.16: Student Council Wants You to Disagree With Administration

You have been asked to be an adviser to the student council. During one grueling session on policies, a few of the brightest council members back you into a corner. They ask your opinion on a particular policy, which the administration condones, but you individually condemn.

What will your reaction to the students be? Choose the best of the following responses:

1. Give the students your opinion and explain how it differs from the administrative response.
2. Give your view without contrasting it to the administrative response.
3. Hedge and throw the matter back to the council at large.
4. Ignore the issue and ask that the topic be dropped—plead the Fifth.

Case 3.16: Rationales for the Alternative Responses

1. This sends straight signals to the students. However, it is not necessary to contrast the views. This could have the effect of making you appear to enjoy challenging authority. Find a better response.
2. This is the best response. You are honest with yourself and others. Your speaking out is in the best democratic tradition, and the school claims that it is educating students to be democratic citizens. You will be a good example for the students.
3. This "gets the monkey off your back" and means you will not have to give emotional resources to potential conflict. However, you will not sense your own efficacy, and the students will see a poor example of leadership. Try another response.
4. This approach also saves resources and will not get you in trouble with the administration. Once again, however, you will not sense your own efficacy and will set a poor example of leadership for your students.

Case 3.17: Monitoring the Restrooms

You are a fifth-grade teacher in a 350-student school. A few fifth-grade boys urinate in sinks, throw wet toilet paper onto the ceiling, put paper towels in the commodes, and have bowel movements in the urinals. The school custodians have had enough; one threatens to quit if he has to clean up any more messes like these. The principal comes to your room angry. "You're going to have to talk to these boys about what happened, and if it happens again there are going to be severe consequences," she says.

What will you do? Please choose the best of the following options:

1. Go the principal's office at the first opportunity and apologize for not having better control over your fifth-grade students.
2. Meet with the other fifth-grade teacher. (There are only two of you.) Have a meeting with the fifth-grade boys and tell them how you feel and what the consequences are for such actions.
3. Meet with the other fifth-grade teacher. Have a meeting with the fifth-grade boys and tell them how you feel. Then have the custodian describe what he has to do to clean up the mess. Tell the boys the consequences for their actions: They'll have to clean up the mess and also clean up the grounds around the school for 2 weeks.
4. Do 3 (above) and also establish a network, whereby boys report things that are severe enough that an adult needs to know about them.
5. Go through the moves to satisfy the principal, but in fact ignore the situation and go about your business.

Case 3.17: Rationales for the Alternative Responses

1. The principal's anger is directed at you for not creating the appropriate climate in terms of discipline. It is important to accept responsibility for this matter. However, this does little to solve the problem, other than letting you vent your guilt. And in fact, you can't monitor the boys' rest-

rooms all of the time and may not have known of such behavior until the principal brought it to your attention. Seek a better response.

2. It is important to involve the other fifth-grade teacher. To meet with boys and girls could turn the session into a silly time. Therefore, meeting with the boys and laying down the law and consequences is a wise move. This is a good response, but it doesn't have any mechanism for reporting offenses. Furthermore, it doesn't assure that the boys understand the burden this places on the custodian. Find a better response.

3. This response has the advantages of 2 (above). It also involves the janitor and lets him tell how he feels about the situation, and it lets the boys know what a burden they are placing on the janitor. You still have not created a mechanism for finding out who the offenders are. Try to find a better response.

4. This response has the advantages of 3 (above) and it also creates a mechanism for finding out who the offenders are. Some critics will say that you are creating snitches or tattletales, but it is important to make a distinction between a person who tells on others about anything and everything, as opposed to a person who reports things severe enough to warrant telling an adult. This is the best response.

5. This approach takes less resources than any of the other approaches. You go on automatic pilot and pretend to go along with the principal, even though you won't really do anything about the matter. After all, these kinds of things happen in schools from time to time. Boys will be boys. The downside of this response is that you will not exercise your responsibility as a teacher, will not sense your efficacy or power to make a difference, and the boys will not help create a clean school or learn to accept responsibility for their actions. Find a better response.

Case 3.18: Breaking Up a Fight

Fights sometimes occur in your school. They are often brought from the neighborhood into the school. One of the things you have discovered is that some students prefer to fight at school because they know adults will break it up; whereas, if the fight took place at a park or shopping center, it could lead to serious physical harm or even death. As one student said, "I fight at school if I want to make a point." The student could "make a point" and still be assured of no serious harm. When a fight occurs, an audience quickly gathers for free entertainment.

A colleague who is an old-timer warns you about breaking up fights: "Watch out for the 'roundhouse right.' This isn't a boxing match where they just throw punches straight at each other. You need peripheral vision."

There is an automatic 3-day suspension for fighting. The only flexibility in this matter is if the adult (or adults) who witnesses the fight judges that a student acted purely in self-defense as a response to assault.

You are getting ready to teach your class after lunch when you hear a commotion in the hall, and a student screams "Fight!" You look in the direction of the noise and see two large boys fighting. What will your response be? Please choose from the following responses:

1. Return to your room, close the door, and let someone else deal with the matter.
2. Go toward the fight and do whatever you can to break it up. Then take the boys to the principal's office.
3. Go toward the fight and do whatever you can to break it up. On your way ask a student to go to the principal's office to tell the principal or assistant principal that a fight is occurring. Help take the boys to the principal's office.
4. Go toward the fight and do whatever you can to break it up. On your way ask a student to go to the principal's office

to tell the principal or assistant principal that a fight is occurring. Do what you can to disperse the crowd of students watching the fight. Help take the boys to the principal's office.

Case 3.18: Rationales for the Alternative Responses

1. Someone more skilled and comfortable in dealing with fights will show up, thus conserving your resources for teaching. Besides, you could get hurt. However, part of your professional responsibility is dealing with matters such as this. And you will not sense your own efficacy or ability to make a difference by isolating yourself. Find a better response.
2. This is the direct way to deal with the matter. You do not have time to do a lot of things, and so you can break up the fight and get back to your classroom. But, there are other resources you could use. Choose a better response.
3. This response uses the principal and/or assistant principal as a resource. The difficulty is that you have not made an effort to disperse the crowd, some of whom could get involved in the fight itself. Find a better response.
4. This response has all of the advantages of responses 2 and 3 (above) and also deals with the difficult issue of crowd control. It is probably the best of the four responses.

Case 3.19: Student Brings Gun to School

Your principal is concerned about facts he received at a recent education association meeting: Every school day at least 100,000 students tote guns in school; 160,000 skip classes because they fear physical harm; 40 are hurt or killed by firearms; 6,250 teachers are threatened with bodily injury; and 260 are physically assaulted. Your principal talks about a West Coast school system that has set up an 800 number so that weapons on campus can be reported anonymously, has banned backpacks, has installed $2,000 metal detectors at school entrances, and has purchased X-ray machines that cost $20,000 each. The goal, according to the principal, is to provide safety comfort zones for students and faculty. The principal shares these facts with teachers in the faculty meeting, and a discussion ensues about the implications of these facts for your school.

The principal's speech comes home for you later in the year. A student bursts into your class first thing in the morning and says that a small group of boys is excitedly milling around a wastebasket in the restroom. The wastebasket has a gun in it. (According to school board policy, students are suspended for the remainder of the year for bringing guns to school.) What will you do?

1. Talk to the boys and find out who threw the gun into the wastebasket. Take that boy and the wastebasket with the gun in it to the principal's office.
2. Take the small group of boys and the wastebasket with the gun in it to the principal's office for further action.
3. Take the gun to the principal's office. Tell the principal what happened.
4. Contact the principal immediately and have the principal deal with the matter.

Case 3.19: Rationales for the Alternative Responses

1. You are on the spot and can find out information immediately. After that you can take the boy who probably brought the gun to the principal's office along with the gun in the wastebasket. It is wise not to handle the gun yourself. But, you can't be sure who brought the gun on the basis of your questioning. And, you may or may not be trained and able to respond effectively. Find a better response.
2. By taking the small group of boys to the principal's office you can keep them from conversing with each other and perhaps blaming the wrong person. This matter is of such importance that the principal, the person officially in charge of the school, should decide what action needs to be taken. You may or may not be trained or able to respond effectively. Seek a better response.

3. This is the direct way to deal with it. It is simple and straightforward. You don't immediately involve others. But, you may or may not be trained or able to respond effectively. Find a better response.

4. There should be a code for a situation like this, a code that was reviewed and practiced at the principal's orientation session in the fall. The principal is the person who should be trained and able to handle situations like this. There should be codes for other matters, too, so that teachers automatically know what to do and where to go. This is the best response.

Case 3.20: Student Brings Drugs to School

Possession of drugs brings an automatic suspension for the remainder of the school year in your school system. While walking down the hall you notice a small group of students near the corner window. Two students in particular catch your attention. They don't see you. One student reaches into a tear on the inside seam of his leather jacket and brings out a small plastic bag of marijuana. You approach the student and take the plastic bag from him. He immediately bolts away from you and runs out the nearest door. What will you do? Please choose the best of the following options:

1. Chase after the student, hoping that you can catch him before he gets too far away. Then bring the student back to the principal's office and tell the principal what happened.

2. Report the matter to the principal's office and wait while the principal calls the student's parent(s).

3. Report the matter to the principal's office and wait while the principal calls the student's parent(s) and the police.

4. Dispose of the plastic bag yourself and hope the matter is over.

Case 3.20: Rationales for the Alternative Responses

1. If you catch the student and bring him to the principal's office, the matter can be handled immediately. Your chances of catching the student run from slim to none. Try a better response.
2. The incident needs to be reported to the principal, the person officially in charge, immediately, and then the principal can notify the parent(s), who will find their son. This response keeps the matter in-house, so that you and the parent(s) can deal with the matter without involving the police. However, the student has violated not only school rules but also the law. Seek a better response.
3. This response covers your school legally and has the advantage that the police can do what is necessary to find the student. This is the best response.
4. This is the quickest response that involves the fewest number of people. However, you will have violated school system policies as well as the law. Find a better response.

Case 3.21: Cheerleader Has Alcohol at Football Game

You are one of the faculty monitors at Friday night football games. While surveying the back of the bleachers and parking lot during halftime, you see a graduate and a student drinking in a car. You knock on the window and ask them to get out of the car. The young woman is a straight-A senior, in her cheerleader's uniform. Your school system's policy is that any student with alcohol on school grounds will automatically receive a 10-day suspension. What will you do? Choose the best of the following options:

1. Talk to the cheerleader and tell her that you are glad you did not see her drinking, because if you had, she would automatically receive a 10-day suspension.

2. Talk to the principal at the first opportunity and tell the principal what you witnessed so that appropriate action can be taken.
3. Talk to the cheerleading coach and let the coach take action, if any is called for in the opinion of the coach.

Case 3.21: Rationales for the Alternative Responses

1. A 10-day suspension will damage the straight-A student's academic record at a time during her senior year when she is applying for colleges. She has made a significant contribution to the school through her good academic work and cheerleading. She is entitled to one mistake. You will also have won a good friend for being flexible. The difficulty with this response is that it plays favorites and supports a kind of entitlement for favored students. Seek a better response.
2. This is the best response. You have assumed your responsibility as a professional and you have not played favorites. If you cannot enforce school policies, you have no business being a monitor at football games. The student may well learn a hard lesson from this experience that will stand her well in the future. It is more important as a professional to be respected than loved.
3. The cheerleading coach is, after all, responsible for the cheerleading squad. It is only fair to tell the coach about this matter. However, you are responsible as a monitor to the principal, but not the cheerleading coach. Find a better response.

4 TEACHER–TEACHER CONFLICT

The world of the elementary-school teacher has, according to educational research, been better described than the world of the secondary-school teacher (Sarason, 1971). This may be in part because the latter is so much larger, more bureaucratized, and more difficult to understand than the former (Sarason, 1971). Both elementary and secondary schools must be understood in terms of the dramatic changes that were "unintended consequences of what was happening in the larger society, not the intended consequences of an articulated policy" (Sarason, 1971, p. 186). For example, the social, ethnic, and cultural composition of people in the cities changed during World War II, when people from rural areas came to the cities to work, and schools reflected the pressures from this change (Sarason, 1971). Likewise, the growth and success of Japanese industries in the past few decades forced American industries, and therefore schools, to question top-down, command-compliance systems for relating to personnel. Decentralization of school system power arrangements, in the name of Site-Based Management, Outcome-Based Education, and the like, were the result.

In spite of new forms of school organization, it is interesting to note how persistent some sources of conflict have been throughout the history of American schools. The cases in this section of the book reflect that persistence.

Inconsistency in Dealing With Students

A constant source of conflict between teachers is the failure on the part of some teachers to discipline students in accordance with written rules, and the obsession of other teachers to discipline students. Some teachers abhor the watchdog function, whereas others delight in it. All teachers are extremely aware of the discipline function, as is noted in the number of cases in this section that deal with the matter of discipline. This is understandable, for throughout the history of schooling, some teachers have always been in danger of losing their jobs because of poor discipline. Stated another way: "Principals give low ratings to teachers who cannot control their classes" (Good & Brophy, 1984, p. 175).

Competition

Another persistent problem in the history of American schools is competition among teachers. The "star system" pits teacher against teacher to win favor from administrators in the school and school system and from parents and students. Unlike the university environment, where professors usually teach a class for 3 hours a week, teachers in schools are with students in a more isolated environment all day long, 5 days a week. Physical proximity is a regularity that creates a kind of intensity among colleagues and students.

There is also a great deal of competition among teachers for the "best" classes and students. More experienced teachers are usually assigned advanced classes, and new teachers are given what are considered less desirable classes. This, incidentally, is one reason for the high turnover among new teachers. There is also competition for the best instructional materials, for example, books. A new teacher complained that all the good textbooks had been checked out by experienced teachers at the first day's orientation. The new teachers didn't even know where the books were kept. Competition for certain rooms, for use of the photocopy machine, library books, in-class personal computers, and instructional software can be intense.

Competition also frequently exists between young teachers and those who are older. Older teachers often resent the pushiness of new teachers, and new teachers in turn accuse older teachers of a reluctance to innovate. Young teachers often feel they are better prepared for teaching because they are acquainted, through recent course work, with the newest trends in thought. Older teachers cite teaching experience as their strong point— something young teachers do not as yet have. Because most school systems honor seniority, young teachers sometimes resent the fact that more experienced teachers have special privileges— such as being asked to serve on the most important committees and getting more pay for experience, rather than merit teaching.

Competition also exists between faculty members representing different areas of the curriculum. In some high schools, mainly suburban schools where the majority of students go on to college, liberal arts teachers look disparagingly on those teaching vocational courses. Some suburban schools were formerly rural schools. While the school was a rural one, the agricultural teacher had a great deal of prestige. His prestige diminished when the school became suburban, and he was assigned gardening classes for future suburban home owners. In some schools athletic coaches have a good deal of prestige; in others, their prestige is lower than that of first-rate teachers who prepare students for college. In short, parents assign prestige to teachers who meet the needs that parents perceive for their children. It is interesting to see how parents want their children to begin playing the next role they anticipate. For example, the preschooler is expected to read and write, and some college preparatory students begin in high school to dress like university students.

All teachers compete for the time of students. Those teachers who assign a large amount of homework and work with the students a great deal in extracurricular areas are frequently resented by other teachers. In a high school setting, the drama teacher may work with students 3 hours an afternoon or evening in order to prepare for the next play; the coach may take athletes away from school for athletic events; and the yearbook or student newspaper sponsor may also demand a great deal of time from students. Any request for the students' time that is out of the ordinary is suspect and exposes the teacher to criticism from colleagues.

Different students appeal to different types of teachers. One teacher's favorite student will be another teacher's problem student. Teachers, naturally thinking that other teachers react to students as they do, defend some students and disparage others, with much of this conflict occurring in the teachers' lounge or lunchroom. Once again, proximity of members of the school as a social system lends itself to such conflict. There is a good deal of backbiting in some schools. Teachers talk about one another in front of fellow teachers, administrators, and at times, students. If administrators employ favoritism, teachers become jealous of the favorite.

There seems to be a strong feeling among teachers that each teacher should carry a fair load of work. Some teachers teach subjects that seem to demand little preparation and no extra time for grading written work. This is resented by teachers who feel their teaching demands more preparation and grading of students' writing.

Finally, there is, on some faculties, conflict between teachers because of racial and ethnic backgrounds. Cliques sometimes form, with a type of de facto segregation taking place in the lunchroom and at social events. Ageism and sexism also cause conflict between teachers. Those near retirement may at times get the feeling that their talents are no longer appreciated. Both women and men may sense exclusion from certain leadership positions because of their gender. And female teachers with children often feel that their role as mothers is not understood or appreciated by some male teachers. Often, teachers who make insensitive remarks are simply not aware of the discriminatory nature of their comments.

Conclusion

Faculty relationships can be very fulfilling, thus negating much of the loneliness that teachers often experience. Being part of an instructional team that is functioning well can be one of teaching's greatest benefits. Such teamwork depends on an honest and open recognition of colleagues' talents and hard work. When a team is working together well, there is a celebration of each person's contributions. The challenge for each teacher is to know oneself and one's colleagues well enough so that diversity is seen as a strength rather than something to just be tolerated.

Case 4.1: You Are Asked to Assess a "Star Teacher" on Your Team

You are new to the school and are asked to join a team of teachers. On your team there is a veteran teacher who is treated as a "star teacher" by the principal and many of the teachers in the school. You notice that this teacher's "stardom" is the result of several factors: The teacher sings in the church choir of a leading church in the city and is a leader in that church; the teacher volunteers for many committees in the school system and serves as the central office's demonstration teacher for workshops; the teacher dresses very well; and the teacher has excellent public relations skills with parents and others in the community.

However, you also notice that the teacher almost never teaches. That is, the teacher writes assignments on the board, which keep the students busy, but rarely teaches the subject matter content and does not grade the students' work in completing the assignments. The "star teacher" does not record grades in the grade book but instead gives the students nothing lower than a C, even though many of the students do not know the material and should receive failing marks. Parents do not complain because their children get good grades.

The "star teacher" recently won the school system's Teacher of the Year award, which consisted of a certificate, press coverage, and $5,000. Last year she was a finalist for the Language Arts Teacher of the Year award, although language arts was taught only three times during the year—the days the teacher was observed by the central office language arts consultant.

The "star teacher" is presently up for the Social Studies Teacher of the Year award. The only time social studies was taught during the first 6 months of the school year was the day the principal did the formal evaluation of the teacher. On that day, the teacher reached into the cupboard and distributed American Indian costumes that the children used to act out a role-playing exercise.

The social studies consultant from central office asks you to come to the central office to give testimony that will be useful in assessing the "star" teacher's teaching.

What will your response be?

(extreme response) Progressive	*neutral*	*(extreme response)* Essentialist
A professional's autonomy is the basis for creativity. The "star teacher," however, is not being creative, but is probably lazy and perhaps incompetent. Professionals have a code of conduct and means for censuring colleagues who abuse such a code. It is your responsibility to give honest testimony to the central office consultant for social studies.		This is precisely the problem with progressivism. The "star teacher" has abused academic freedom to do whatever the teacher wants to do. There are no checks in place to keep this teacher in line. The only honest thing to do is to give accurate testimony to the central office consultant. This increases the chances of this teacher's "shaping up or shipping out" so that a competent teacher who knows the subject matter will be hired.

Case 4.2: You Are Puzzled as to How to Relate to a Superior Teacher

As a recent university graduate you entered teaching, hoping to make a real difference in the lives of students. The teacher in the room next to you is truly a superior teacher, due to a combination of factors: high energy level, love of students and teaching, high but realizable expectations for students, expertise or competence in the subjects taught, and the ability to use many and varied teaching techniques.

You experience difficulty in relating to this teacher on two different levels. You wonder about your teaching style compared to the superior teacher's style, and you favor the essentialist philosophy of teaching, whereas the superior teacher favors the progressive philosophy of teaching.

You ask yourself: "What steps can I take to reconcile this dilemma?" You are starting to lose sleep over the matter—particularly since the superior teacher's work is so obvious to you because you are in adjacent classrooms. How will you respond to this situation?

(extreme response) Progressive	neutral	*(extreme response)* Essentialist
This case proves the very real problem the essentialist has in not giving enough attention to teaching processes. The superior teacher is superior because the teacher is willing to use anything and everything to teach effectively. If the essentialist-oriented beginning teacher is really concerned, it would be wise to mimic the superior teacher briefly and then branch off to a creative style of his or her own.		You and the superior teacher have different basic assumptions about what teaching should be. As an essentialist, you are committed to teaching that passes on the essentialist heritage of your knowledge area. Other goals must be aligned with this basic assumption. Your teacher-centered instruction must also be aligned with this assumption, so do not concern yourself with emulating the superior teacher's progressive instructional techniques. Trust your own judgment on this matter. That teacher's other personal and professional traits, such as a high energy level and manifest love of students, might be worth emulation, however.

Case 4.3: Your Reaction When Another Teacher Changes His or Her Curriculum

You learn from a third party that a fellow teacher is omitting from his or her course a chapter normally covered in the course. There are 10 weeks left in the school year.

What is your reaction?

(extreme response) Progressive	neutral	(extreme response) Essentialist
A professional's autonomy is the basis for creativity. The teacher is certainly within his or her rights to drop a chapter if, according to his or her professional judgment, it is in the interest of the learner to do so. Therefore, simply go about your business unless it seems appropriate to reinforce your colleague's professional judgment. (That is, offer support for and approval of his or her judgment.)		The essential content for the course has been set and a deviation from it violates the original intent of those who set the curriculum. The only legitimate reason for changing content is if it is not consistent with the essentialist position of passing along basic knowledge. Use whatever influence you have to get the maverick teacher back on track so that the essentialist position is conserved (and therefore the students' interests are properly served).

Case 4.4: Mentor Questions Possible Innovation

You are a relatively new teacher whose mentor is very "traditional"—a 30-year veteran. When you are discussing teaching the concept of the seven continents and their location, you mention that you are considering using a hands-on approach, by letting your students make globes of their own and place the continents on them.

Your mentor tells you that this is a waste of valuable instructional time and she recommends a worksheet on the same concept.

What will your reaction be?

(extreme response) Progressive	neutral	(extreme response) Essentialist
Thank her for her advice and take the worksheet. Then, in your classroom, you teach the concept with your hands-on approach, and later use her worksheet to see if it assesses how your students mastered the concept.		The mentor is correct to question frills that may well take students' attention away from the essential knowledge that must be learned. More active student involvement, such as making a globe, will obviously consume more instructional time; hence, it is not the most efficient use of instructional time. Reconsider your plan in light of essentialist principles.

Case 4.5: Teacher Tries to Override Your Judgment

As an eighth-grade teacher, it is your responsibility to make mathematics recommendations for your students entering the ninth grade. A teacher in another grade level tutors two of your students privately. In your opinion, these two students need to repeat Algebra I in the ninth grade, as they have barely passed the class. Their "tutor" recommends that they should go on to geometry. She says that if they take her special 3-week algebra review tutorial in the summer, they will be ready.

What will your reaction be?

(extreme response) Progressive	neutral	(extreme response) Essentialist
Talk to the teacher ("tutor") as a fellow professional and express your reservations about the students' readiness to take geometry. Discuss data surrounding the students' performance. Support the 3-week tutorial if the students and their parents wish to pursue it, and let the students take their chances in ninth grade geometry.		Talk to the parents and give them all of the facts. Tell them you have serious doubts that a 3-week course is sufficient enough to build a strong foundation to master basic algebraic concepts and skills. You may wish to talk to the principal, asking if the teacher's ("tutor's") methods are ethical.

Case 4.6: Teacher's Reaction to Implementing New Program

You are one of the three teachers at your school who teach on the same grade level. System wide, your grade level is asked to restructure your classrooms, using more developmentally appropriate teaching methods. The grade level chairman devises a plan for the next school year, and you all agree to try it.

After teaching for 4 months using this method, you realize that you are not obtaining the results you have hoped for. You mention this in a grade level meeting, and the chairperson becomes very defensive. Later, in private, the other teacher says she is having similar problems, but she will not bring it up in front of the grade level chairperson.

What will you do?

(extreme response) *Progressive*	*neutral*	(extreme response) *Essentialist*
Continue to use basically the same format, but adjust it to accommodate your teaching style and students. Explain this to the grade level chairperson and tell her that next year you will be glad to use the same curriculum, but you will not be using the same method because it does not work as well for you as it does for her.		Stop the method immediately and return to a method that embodies essentialist tenets. Such a method would be focused more on the basic knowledge to be imparted than on new methods of teaching that might be deemed developmentally appropriate.

**Case 4.7: You Experience Disagreement With Some
Colleagues Regarding Basic Assumptions
Underlying an Educational Reform Project**

You are one of five faculty members from your school attending an educational reform conference sponsored by the private foundation that has funded innovative projects in 10 schools throughout the nation. The format for the morning session at the conference is as follows: (a) a speech by a well-known consultant on "the creation of educational settings" and (b) five-person discussion groups with one person from each funded project in each of the 10 groups.

The speaker begins by saying that many, if not most, people in an innovative project are in denial much of the time. They prefer to get on "the arc of optimism," rather than facing very real problems in the creation of an educational setting. The speaker cites the work of Yale psychologist Seymour Sarason in general and *The Creation of Settings and the Future Societies* in particular. The speaker agrees with Sarason that it is during the "honeymoon" period that participants in the creation of a setting must sit down and talk about possible problems.

The speaker then talks about our fear of death, something we become conscious of at about 3 years of age, causing us to create all kinds of denial mechanisms that keep us from dealing with reality. In particular, we turn our attention to "the heroic," rather than doing the hard work required of us in facing the reality that all innovative projects rise and fall (die). The speaker concludes with a warning that public relations leaders will try to "put a positive spin" on everything, which in fact amounts to a denial of reality. The speaker encourages participants to face reality and share the good and the bad with the public. To do so is to be authentic rather than phony. And, as Erving Goffman says in his classic work on leadership, *The Presentation of Self in Everyday Life,* authenticity is the key to effectiveness.

It is clear from the nonverbal cues of your fellow faculty members that you have reacted positively to many of the speaker's points, whereas they have reacted negatively and vice versa.

You are now in your small group, and discussion begins. What will you say in reaction to the speaker's comments?

(extreme response) Progressive	neutral	*(extreme response)* Essentialist
The speaker has given us some helpful hints in creating learning settings. As progressives we have sometimes been betrayed by "disciples" who distort our ideas to mean that anything goes. The challenge is to communicate to others those values that are part of the progressive tradition. One of these values is genuineness and authenticity. In fact, these values are central to the humanistic tradition in education.		The speaker speaks the truth. As with teaching, there are certain essentials in the creation of other settings, such as the need for authenticity, and if these essentials are ignored, the project is doomed. Grief is a natural response to things having gone wrong, and to grieve is to share reality with others. Grief is a part of literature, music, and drama. The speaker challenges us to look inside of ourselves and draw on our integrity, rather than to hire "spin doctors" and other consultants who put icing on the cake instead of simply creating an excellent cake out of essential ingredients. One must be honest about the pros and cons of any education initiative.

Case 4.8: Colleague Criticizes Your Teaching

You are a teacher, and it comes to your attention that the teacher in the room next to you is making negative comments to students, the principal, other teachers, and parents regarding your teaching. Furthermore, you hear that this colleague sometimes allows gossip about teachers in class.

What will you do? Please choose the best response from the following alternatives:

1. Point out in a firm but polite way that there are many and diverse teaching styles, with no one style "right" for all teachers.
2. Ignore the colleague's comments and go about your business, continuing to use your present approach to teaching.
3. Say to this colleague that you disagree with the criticism, but are fair-minded enough to want the advice of others. Say that you are willing to have your colleague air the criticism in front of the principal and/or teachers' advisory council.
4. Confront your colleague by saying that critics who dish it out should also be able to take it. Lambaste the critic's teaching.
5. Take this matter to the principal.

Case 4.8: Rationales for the Alternative Responses

1. This response has the advantage of leaving you with the feeling that you are honestly stating your view. Your colleague cannot fault you for being deceitful. But it is not a good first response because you do not know for sure if the rumors you have heard are true. You may well appear to be "coming out of the blue" to the teacher.
2. This is the best initial response. You need to check out the rumors if you wish to escalate to another response, such as 1 and/or 3. This response will buy you time.
3. This is a good strategy for "smoking out" a critic who is talking behind your back. However, it is to be saved for those rare occasions when nothing else seems to get the

critic in line. It will probably have the effect of quieting the critic because he or she will know you are aware of what is going on. Consider a better opening response.

4. This certainly gets it out front. It is true that those who dish it out should also be able to take it. However, this strategy is also a strategy of last resort. Try another response.

5. This can have the effect of quieting the critic. The critic must respond to someone with higher positional authority. But going to the principal can give you the reputation of being a tattletale. Also, this is a tacit admission that you cannot handle the problem and instead need to solicit the help of someone with positional authority. That could be interpreted as a sign of weakness. Consider a better response.

Case 4.9: Colleagues Critical of Teacher

You have just completed your second year of teaching and begin to hear rumors that the teachers at the grade level above you are dissatisfied with the qualifications of the students they have received from your previous classes.

Rumors have it that, during conferences with parents, teachers are critical of you and your teaching style. When students have difficulty adjusting to their teaching styles and expectations, teachers place the blame on you.

What will you do? Please choose from the following responses:

1. Confront the teachers and insist that they detail their criticisms. Then defend your methods and practices.

2. Talk to the principal about this matter and go on from there.

3. Ignore the rumors and go about your business.

Case 4.9: Rationales for the Alternative Responses

1. This approach has the advantage of clearing the air quickly. The teachers in the grade level above you may be angry at

you, but they cannot honestly call you deceitful. Clearly stating your defense is also straightforward and to the point. The difficulty with this strategy is that it is confrontational and you have not checked out the rumors to be sure they are accurate. Consider a better response.

2. You can use the principal's positional authority to deal with this matter. However, you may get the reputation of being a tattletale, and it is a tacit admission that you cannot deal with a problem. This might serve to lower the principal's professional opinion of you.

3. This is probably the best approach for the moment. If rumors persist, adopt strategy 1 and/or 2.

Case 4.10: Conduct in the Hall and Cafeteria

There is a school rule against running in the hallways, and students are supposed to behave properly in the cafeteria during lunchtime.

A teacher consistently fails to enforce rules. During the lunch period, this teacher turns her back to the students she is supposed to supervise and talks to the custodians. A first-year teacher starts to emulate the teacher who ignores rules, and the cafeteria is gradually going out of control.

What will you do? Please choose the best of the following responses:

1. Talk to the colleague who is not doing the job and point out that you and your colleagues are not being treated fairly in covering for that teacher.
2. Ignore the colleague's behavior and simply do the best you can under the circumstances.
3. Take this matter to the principal.
4. Take this matter to the faculty advisory council.
5. Talk to a teacher who is a close friend of the teacher not doing the supervisory work. Ask the friend to intercede.

Case 4.10: Rationales for the Alternative Responses

1. This is a direct and honest response. The colleague cannot fairly say that you are guilty of duplicity.
2. This is probably the best initial response. If the colleague's behavior continues to be unacceptable you would be wise to escalate to 1, 3, or 4.
3. You can use the positional authority of the principal to bring the colleague in line. However, you may well get the reputation as a tattletale. Try another response.
4. This is professional censure, which is the last resort, but a sometimes necessary resort, for the teacher as a professional. It will in effect probably shame the colleague. The downside of this response, rather obviously, is that it backs the colleague into a corner, so that it is difficult to save face. Try another response.
5. The word will certainly get to your colleague who is out of line. And it will be delivered by someone who matters to the colleague. However, it appears as if you are afraid to talk to the colleague yourself. Therefore, try another response.

Case 4.11: Conflict With Teacher Who Keeps Students After the Bell

You are a new teacher in a school that operates on the bell system. Students are late to your class because one teacher consistently keeps students past the time when the bell rings to signal the end of class.

What will you do? Please choose the best of the following responses:

1. Talk to the colleague who is keeping the students after the bell. The colleague may not be aware of the problem.
2. Ignore the colleague's behavior and simply do the best you can under the circumstances.
3. Take this matter to the principal.

   4. Take this matter to the faculty advisory council.
   5. Put pressure on the students to put pressure on their teacher.

Case 4.11: Rationales for the Alternative Responses

   1. This is probably the best response. The colleague may simply be wrapped up in the instructional process and is therefore not aware of the annoyance caused.
   2. This avoids the possibility of conflict with your colleague. However, it does not solve the problem and does not give you a release for your feelings. Try another response.
   3. It surely is one way to get the teacher in line quickly. But, it is probably overkill and will give you the reputation of a tattletale and an overreactor. Find a better response.
   4. This is also a quick way to get the message to the teacher. However, it has the disadvantages detailed in 3, above.
   5. This may well accomplish your objective of making the teacher more sensitive to the bell. However, it puts the students in the middle and is using the students to get what you want. Try another response.

Case 4.12: Your Reaction to Teachers' Objections to Your Proposed Field Trip

   You are planning to take your students to see a play in a local theater—a play the class is currently studying. The class is looking forward to the performance, and you have secured the permission of the administration and the parents. However, some fellow teachers object to this field trip because students will be absent from their classes that day. They suggest that you cancel the field trip in order to prevent discord among the faculty.

   What will you do? Please choose the best of the following responses:

   1. Cancel your plans in the interest of good relations with your colleagues who have complained.

2. Ignore the colleagues' remarks and simply do what you think is right—go to the play.
3. Take this matter to the principal for advice.
4. Try to reschedule this trip for a Saturday or a school holiday.
5. Take the matter to the faculty advisory council as quickly as possible.

Case 4.12: Rationales for the Alternative Responses

1. Your colleagues' opinion of you is an important matter. You want to appear to be a good team player. But, you have worthy instructional objectives for this field trip that would not be met. Consider other responses.
2. This is the best response. Colleagues take students to a variety of out-of-school activities. You are only going to be absent for one day, and it is a worthwhile activity.
3. The principal can bring about quick action because of positional authority. However, it would appear to be overkill, and you would appear to need help from above. Choose a better response.
4. This would be one way to avoid conflict and loss of approval from colleagues. However, it would inconvenience you and your students, some of whom have other commitments, such as work, on Saturdays. Find a better response.
5. This is another way to bring pressure to bear on colleagues, but the response seems to be stronger than you need for going to the play. Choose a better response.

Case 4.13: Colleague Assigns a Great Deal of Homework

A colleague assigns a great deal of homework, and students complain to you that they don't have time to do the homework you assign because of this. One day a student, who says she has been designated to speak for the class, asks you in front of the entire class if you can do something about this matter.

What will you do? Please choose the best of the following alternatives:

1. Talk to colleagues and ask for advice.
2. Speak to the teacher who assigns a great deal of homework. The colleague may not know the hardship this imposes on the students and you.
3. Say nothing and simply do the best you can under the circumstances.
4. Talk to the principal about the matter.
5. Take the homework assignment problem to the faculty advisory council, but do not single out the teacher in question.

Case 4.13: Rationales for the Alternative Responses

1. Colleagues can sometimes give you insights into why faculty members do certain things. The problem is that this approach will probably not influence the teacher in question to do anything. Also, in the event that the word gets back to the teacher, you may be criticized for not being more direct. Choose another response.
2. This approach is direct and honest and will certainly get the attention of the colleague. However, our experience tells us that most teachers will not be persuaded by another colleague on the homework matter. Try another response.
3. This will provoke no one. However, it doesn't address the problem, which will probably persist. You might also lose some respect from students for being too reticent. Try another response.
4. Go to the top to get action. We know this works but you will be known as a tattletale if this gets back to the teacher. This also lets the principal know that you cannot handle a rather common problem among faculty members. Seek another response.
5. This is probably the best response. There will be a professional decision that will serve as advice to all faculty. The advisory council will deliver this advice at a faculty meeting or in a memo. If this doesn't work, you need to consider other stronger responses.

Case 4.14: Teacher Leaves Your Classroom in a Mess

Teachers must move from classroom to classroom in your school because of a lack of classroom space. One teacher leaves your classroom in a mess, with chairs and tables changed around and not moved back before you teach. Desks are written on, used gum is stuck on the bottom of desks, and paper is scattered on the floor.

What will you do? Please choose the best of the following responses:

1. Talk to the teacher privately and explain what the problem is and your reaction to it; namely, the hardship that it works on you and your students.
2. Ignore the problem and simply go about your business.
3. Take this matter to the principal for advice and action.
4. Talk to colleagues and ask for advice.
5. Talk to custodians and ask for advice.

Case 4.14: Rationales for the Alternative Responses

1. This approach is direct and honest and therefore the best. It has the advantage that you will either deal with the matter to your satisfaction or you can escalate to another option if this does not work.
2. You will not get anybody mad with this strategy. However, you will not address the problem and you will not release your feelings. Try another response.
3. The principal has the positional authority to get a quick response. But you will be known as a tattletale if you do this very often. And it has the usual disadvantage of admitting tacitly that you cannot handle the problem. Consider other responses.
4. Colleagues can give you good information and also provide emotional support. However, they will probably tell the teacher in question and you will be known for not being direct. Choose a better response.

5. Custodians and secretaries really run schools, according to many who know. However, custodians are not supervisors of teachers, and so this strategy probably will not work. Consider a better response.

Case 4.15: Flighty Teacher Drives Team Members Crazy

You are a member of a teaching team that has been to conferences on collaborative teaching, integrated curriculum, site-based management, and multi-aged grouping. Your teaching team has correlated many of the key organizing concepts from these innovations into what you feel is a conceptually sound instructional program.

The difficulty is one member of your teaching team whose flighty behavior is driving other team members crazy. The difficult team member is congenial and cooperative. However, this flighty person engages in a number of disruptive and unprofessional practices. For example, first thing each morning this team member wears a Walkman to listen to a disc jockey's quiz program. Suddenly, sometimes during a lesson, the teacher will ask you to take over so that a call can be made to the radio station to try to win the morning's jackpot. The team member asks you to watch for the principal, so that the teacher's headset can be taken off at a moment's notice.

What will you do? Please choose the best option from the following alternatives:

1. Confront the teacher about this matter of unprofessional practices.
2. Take the matter to other team members informally to solicit their advice.
3. Talk to the principal and seek advice as to what can be done.
4. Write an anonymous note about this matter and send it to the principal.
5. Take this matter to the next team meeting and discuss it as a team. Be diplomatic.
6. Do nothing at all, since all of us have idiosyncrasies.

Case 4.15: Rationales for the Alternative Responses

1. This is an honest and direct approach. It is probably the best initial response you can make. You are assuming your professional responsibility, and the problem is a rather serious breach of professional practices. If this doesn't work, try 5 as a good second choice.

2. You often learn a great deal through informal communication. However, this makes you appear to be a gossip who will not confront the teacher directly. Choose another response.

3. Once again, you will get quick action from someone with positional authority over the teacher. But, you will be known as a tattletale. Moreover, the teacher will also probably get into a great deal of difficulty with the principal over this matter. Try another response.

4. This can be an effective approach in getting the message across, but it is considered less than direct and deceitful by many people. Consider other responses.

5. The teaching team can make things happen in a small community or group setting. It is a fine example of professional decision making. This is a good second choice, but consider other options at this time.

6. It is true that all of us have idiosyncrasies. However, this teacher's behavior is unprofessional, and therefore you should consider other options.

5 ADMINISTRATOR– TEACHER CONFLICT

Administrators are usually former teachers who have changed roles (Sarason, 1971). Promising young teachers frequently look to administrative positions as part of their career patterns. The community at large and other members of the school as a social system anticipate such mobility. Failure to recognize important differences in the roles of teachers and administrators, as well as incompetent people sometimes playing administrative roles, is a source of conflict between teachers and administrators. Seymour Sarason argues that there is a tendency to overevaluate the power of the principal, much as we do the president of the United States (Sarason, 1971).

Administrators Too Sensitive to the Public

Part of the folklore of the teaching profession is the story of the principal reprimanding the teacher because of one parent's phone call. This illustrates the commonplace teachers' view that administrators are much too sensitive to the public. Administrators in turn talk about the naïvete of teachers in not recognizing the influence of the public on the schools. Without the support of the public, it is argued, administrators are in peril of losing their jobs. When a new administration enters a school system or school, there is a honeymoon period, but as soon as the new administration starts making decisions that influence the children of the school, some parents will be angry, pressing for the dismissal of the newly formed administration.

Although principals act in part as buffers of criticism aimed at teachers, some teachers make serious mistakes—mistakes that often come to the immediate attention of the principal through a single phone call. In such cases the teacher must be conferred with for the benefit of the students.

Teachers, claiming that administrators are public relations persons rather than educational leaders, criticize administrators for impeding progress by stifling innovation. The administrator who decides to innovate needs the support of teachers.

Too Much Busywork

Teachers, like their students and some administrators, complain about the excessive amount of busywork or petty tasks they are required to perform. Teachers are frequently asked to collect lunch money, supervise the cafeteria, sell insurance to students, and fill out a multitude of forms throughout the day. Much of the conflict between teachers and administrators focuses on the amount of life space administrators have, compared to teachers. This conflict is symbolized by the fact that the principal has a phone, a secretary, and the freedom to leave the school almost at will. Teachers, on the other hand, are confined to the classroom (Sarason, 1971).

The school, in order to protect itself from public criticism, requires evidence in writing at nearly every step of the educational process. The results of this are evident in the commonly heard remark that teachers are baby-sitters.

Related to this issue is the matter of the incongruous roles teachers are often expected to play. The teacher is supposed to be a scholar, a teacher, and a policeman. The watchdog role frequently expected of teachers is demonstrated to an extreme degree by the principal who suggested that teachers crawl up into trees at the rear of the building to take pictures of smokers. In this way there would be clear-cut evidence of rule violation. In a high school, the principal assigned men teachers to foot patrol the student parking lot at lunchtime to deter fights and to see that smoking, drug use, and sexual activity did not go on in students' cars.

Teachers often feel that administrators do not understand the academic role teachers are expected to play, since administrators are not scholars in the minds of teachers but primarily public relations persons. Teachers frequently see themselves as political pawns for administrators who are out for their own political gain.

In short, many teachers feel that our schools are obsessed with trivia at the expense of the major goal our schools should have—that is, the creation of an atmosphere in which students learn. Classroom interruptions, in the form of suddenly called assemblies, public address announcements, and taking students from class for club pictures, make teachers antagonistic toward administrators.

Discipline

Going to school is compulsory; teacher-student ratios are high; and philosophies on discipline are multifarious. These factors help account for the existence of discipline problems and also for their perpetuation. It is little wonder, then, that discipline is a source of irritation between administrators and teachers. Each is subjected to criticism by the other on this issue: Some are considered too easy on the students; others are considered drillmasters; and still others are considered out of touch with modern learning theory. Teachers frequently say that administrators do not support them in discipline matters, while principals complain that teachers are not skilled in handling behavior problems (Jones, 1987).

A behavior problem that provokes disciplinary action by the teacher, which is challenged outside the school, often brings tension into the teacher-administrator relationship. Administrators usually give vocal support to their teachers prior to such incidents. However, they often appear to support the superintendent and board of education rather than teachers after a conflict situation arises. This, among other reasons, is why teachers feel administrators are engaged in duplicity, thus creating a gap between administrative rhetoric and reality.

The Power Differential

There is a sense in which the principal cannot win with teachers: Teachers want to feel a closeness with the principal and yet feel threatened when such closeness occurs, because of the position of authority the principal has over teachers. Teachers sometimes claim administrators are not accessible to teachers, and yet the same teachers complain of snooping and micro-managing when they feel the administrators are spending too much time around their classrooms or in the teachers' lounge.

The administration has a great deal of power over teachers, thus accounting for much of the anxiety teachers feel when confronted by administrators. The administration controls the budget, controls the class schedule, sanctions materials used by teachers, offers or fails to offer tenure to new teachers, evaluates all teachers, assigns classes to teachers, and generally runs the school.

Yet it is certainly true that there are many different administrative styles. Some principals coerce their teachers to join a particular union and give their fair share to the charitable causes they support. Other principals refuse to employ such coercive methods. Some principals play favorites with teachers, whereas others do not.

All of these problems and more are the subject of the following cases, which deal with conflict between administrators and teachers.

Case 5.1: Potential Conflict With Principal After Being Named Teacher of the Year Three Times

The neighborhood surrounding the school where you teach has changed from blue-collar suburban to ethnically diverse urban. With the changes in the school, you responded to the principal's desire for a very orderly school by having classes that are always quiet, with students in straight rows. You are clearly in charge of the classroom at all times. The principal holds you up as a model for all teachers but new teachers in particular.

Visitors applaud your classroom management techniques, which makes the principal very happy since the image of the school is uppermost in the principal's mind. You have won the Teacher of the Year award in the school three times during the past 7 years.

One morning you wake up in a cold sweat after having a dream that is in fact more like a nightmare. In this dream a beam of light is directed toward your head, and a voice says "There is more to teaching than keeping order." In thinking about the dream, it seems to you as if the light represents your conscience. Furthermore, you remember your teaching days prior to the principal's clamping down, a time when you used many and diverse teaching methods, rather than simply teacher-directed techniques. You sense a very powerful contradiction: If you change your teaching approach, you will run the risk of losing favor with the principal, and yet you sense that a change would be good for your students and you.

What will you do?

(extreme response) Progressive	neutral	(extreme response) Essentialist
The teaching approach you used prior to your school's becoming urban is consistent with progressive principles. Your experience and conscience tell you that it is time for a change, a change that will make teaching more enjoyable for you and your students. Therefore, you resolve to return to your former teaching approach.		The teaching approach you have used since the school became urban is consistent with essentialist principles. Students learn self-discipline as a result of being in a well-structured environment. This is not the easiest way to teach, but for the good of the students, you must continue to teach as you recently have. After all, it won you much affirmation. Furthermore, you will be probably be further rewarded for this style.

Case 5.2: Principal Wants Curriculum Reform

Your principal has just returned from a week's in-service experience, during which the consultants demonstrated how the Great Books and Socratic method can be linked to make teaching and learning more rational. The Great Books authors include Aristotle, Einstein, Darwin, Machiavelli, Saint Thomas Aquinas, Saint Augustine, and Montaigne. When the principal shows you the list of Great Books, you note that the list includes works by few women and almost no minorities. Your principal defends the list by saying that talk about multiculturalism, "technology-relevant" education, and egalitarian chic supports educational fadism. Your principal has a large poster that quotes St. John's College President Christopher Nelson: "In a rapidly changing world, the least valuable education is one that trains you in something that won't be around tomorrow."

Your principal argues that the Socratic method will teach students to listen well and articulate their views in a public forum—skills that will serve them well as citizens in a democratic society. Furthermore, your principal argues that school attendance will rise, due to the fact that students will have to come to school to keep up with the dialogue.

Finally, the principal says that the basic tenets of the Socratic method and the Great Books approach must be inculcated in the school's curriculum. You are asked to head the committee that will plan for this transition.

What is your reply?

(extreme response) Progressive	neutral	(extreme response) Essentialist
You respectfully decline the offer to head the committee. Or, you agree to head it if the principal will allow you to use your ideas as the committee does its work. You can accept the idea that there are many great books, but the list of Great Books held by your principal is much too narrow, at the expense of women and minorities. It is also too Eurocentric. You can accept the idea that dialogue is important, but you are nervous about such dialogue being teacher-centered. You respect your principal's enthusiasm and should communicate this, but feel an obligation to disagree with course content and teaching style advocated by the principal. You also feel that the principal's ideas should be discussed by the entire faculty *before* a decision is made to move ahead with the principal's plan for Great Books and the initiation of the Socratic method. (The list of authors is too limited and the teaching methodology too teacher-centered.)		You are delighted to be asked to serve as head of the school's curriculum committee that will plan for this transition. The experiences the principal had at the week's seminar on the Great Books and the Socratic method was clearly based on essentialist principles. Students will have a solid knowledge base to react to, and they will be stimulated to know where they and their peers stand on important issues, as a result of the Socratic dialogue.

Case 5.3: Your Reaction to a Proposal for Site-Based Management

Your school year begins with a 3-day retreat. Your principal recently attended a conference on site-based management, along with fellow principals and superintendents in your school system. They agreed that each school in the system should be invited to apply for pilot or experimental status in moving to a site-based management model.

Your principal generally supports the idea, but has some reservations about site-based management. The principal talks about drawbacks with the traditional top-down way of exercising authority in organizations in a new information-age society. The principal also talks about the potential that facilitative power has for professional decision making on the part of teachers and administrators. Facilitative power, according to the principal, is one way to overcome both obvious and not so obvious areas of disagreement in the school. (By facilitative power, the principal means that you bring out the leadership qualities of others, rather than giving them "commands.")

What will your reaction be to the invitation to have your school become a pilot project for site-based management?

(extreme response) Progressive	neutral	(extreme response) Essentialist
The invitation to apply for pilot status in the new site-based management program has tremendous potential for effecting change in the school. Facilitative power is clearly consistent with societal changes in general and the move from an industrial age to an information age society in particular. It is also a sign of hope that professionalism can be enhanced. You must be alert, however, to the possibility that the principal, who is formally designated as the final authority in the school, can take back at any moment power shared with teachers.		The case has two elements that deserve your attention. On the one hand, it is your position that product is more important than process, and site-based management may improve test scores and the like. At the same time, however, facilitative power and site-based management may go too far, so that students challenge teachers' positional authority. You will need to weigh carefully the possible good versus the possible bad in the proposal. Being basically conservative, the essentialist must be wary of mechanisms that so clearly facilitate change. At the same time, the proposal increases one's sense of professionalism.

Case 5.4: Principal Receives Anonymous Note About You

Your principal receives an anonymous note, full of derogatory remarks about you as a teaching professional. He privately reads the contents to you and says that he puts no stock in it. Later, you discover that the principal not only keeps the note and other similar things in his file but uses content from these stored items in subsequent evaluations.

What is your reaction?

(extreme response) Progressive	neutral	(extreme response) Essentialist
Involvement with parents and the community is a basic progressive tenet. Tell the principal that you welcome comments, including complaints, from parents and others and will be happy to discuss these matters with them and him. Make it clear to him that the progressive idea of "creation of community" among faculty and others is impaired by his practice of using anonymous notes and the like against the subject of such notes.		The teacher is a professional whose knowledge of subject matter and teaching is an essential part of the "business" of schools and schooling. Tell the principal that using the contents of anonymous notes is an erosion of professionalism that will not be tolerated by you and fellow professionals. If necessary, pursue the matter with your education association.

Case 5.5: Administrator Holds Tenure Over Your Head

You are codirector of a program for which you are doing half the work. The program requires many hours after school and at night. The other director receives remuneration from the Parent Teacher Association that she doesn't offer to share with you. After the first year, you go to your principal and ask that you also receive some compensation. Your principal tells you that unless you continue to help—for free—you will not be recommended for tenure.

How will you respond?

(extreme response) Progressive	neutral	(extreme response) Essentialist
Continue to help, trying to recall that you originally started because you enjoy children and love to work with them. Work through your education association and other channels, however, to form policies designed to assure equity in compensation for extracurricular or cocurricular programs and activities.		This is an affront to you as a professional who has established authority through your expertise. Do whatever it takes to make it clear that such behavior on the part of the principal is unprofessional. For example, you may wish to have a private conference with the principal, solicit help from your education association, or use grievance appeals channels.

Case 5.6: Administrator Asks You to Do His "Dirty Work"

A teacher on your team is having terrible problems with students and parents. Your principal calls you in and tells you that because you are team leader, you must try to defuse the situation. He says that he is tired of the complaints and will hold you personally responsible if they do not stop.

How will you react?

(extreme response) *Progressive*	*neutral*	*(extreme response)* *Essentialist*
Point out to the principal that the decentralization of authority through teaching teams is consistent with your (progressive) views. Add that you will work with the teacher to improve. However, make it clear that ultimate authority in the school resides with the principal, and he therefore must take some direct responsibility for the supervision of the teacher in question.		This is a good example of the breakdown of schools due to liberal, progressive practices, such as delegating power to teachers that should be kept in the hands of the principal. Do what you can to persuade the principal to assume the authority that he is paid to exercise. Point out that your primary responsibility as a teacher is to impart subject matter, not to take on enhanced administrative functions.

Case 5.7: Administrator Questions Teaching Methods

Through the grapevine, your principal receives some information about your teaching methods that he questions. Instead of coming straight to you, you find out that he is talking to some of your students to try to find out what they think of your teaching practices.

What will you do, if anything?

(extreme response) Progressive	neutral	(extreme response) Essentialist
Talk to the principal, saying that you welcome people to observe your teaching because any professional should be able to explain teaching practices. Through observation and advice, one grows and learns. It will be clear from your comment that the principal's indirect approach to this matter is unprofessional. You have in effect modeled professional leadership behavior for him.		When you were hired, you were hired because of your knowledge of the discipline you are teaching as well as knowledge of teaching practices. Challenge the principal's expertise since he is a manager, not a scholar.

Case 5.8: Principal Assigns You to Lead Workshop
in Traditional Setting

You are a new teacher, recently hired in a school system that follows traditional practices. Many teachers within the system have practiced conservative teaching methods since they were hired many years ago. The principal is very impressed in the interview by your creative and imaginative ideas. The principal requests that you lead a workshop on how you are going to structure your teaching and how your classroom will ensure student learning.

You feel uncomfortable as a newcomer sharing your ideas with veteran teachers, who know much more about the system and students than you do. You also foresee that this workshop could foster resentment and the making of professional adversaries.

What is your response to the principal about leading the workshop?

(extreme response) Progressive	neutral	(extreme response) Essentialist
This is an excellent opportunity to introduce faculty members to your philosophy of teaching—a child-centered one that actively involves all participants in the workshop experience. Try to model progressive practices throughout the workshop. You would be wise to include teacher assistants and other interested adults who can become part of the school community. This is consistent with the progressive belief that the school is a miniature society that reflects the larger society.		This is an excellent opportunity to introduce faculty members to your essentialist views on teaching. You may wish to bring a university professor to the seminar as a guest speaker. You must model the essentialist tenets while conducting the seminar.

Case 5.9: Suspended Student Returns Without Work

One of your students has returned to school without his assigned work after several days of suspension. The principal had asked you to prepare assignments for this student to complete during his suspension. This student has not completed any of the assignments. You go to the principal and explain the situation; he shrugs his shoulders and laughs, as if it were okay that this student has not carried out his responsibilities.

How will you respond?

(extreme response) Progressive	neutral	(extreme response) Essentialist
It is obvious that the principal is "out of the loop" on this matter. Because one of a progressive's tenets is work with parents and the community, it would be wise to contact the parents and call them in for a conference. You can then determine what steps should be taken. The principal's inaction is annoying, but as a professional, you are willing to step into the leadership void and lead.		Administer your own punishment to the student for his failure to complete his work. To pamper this student simply reinforces his inappropriate academic behavior.

Case 5.10: Your Decision on How Best to Teach Students Who Will Not Learn in the Traditional Way

You are teaching in a new school. It is the principal's policy to make three observations of your class during the year. Having three classes of very difficult youngsters, you decide to use the established curriculum as a springboard. The class decides to write plays, journals, short stories, and so on about life as they see it. Your administrator questions you about your decision to change the curriculum.

What is your reaction?

(extreme response) Progressive	neutral	(extreme response) Essentialist
As a professional and a progressive, you can explain what you are doing and why. The key is to provide a rationale for your decision—for you are using the established curriculum as a springboard, rather than throwing it out. There is a good chance you can help your principal understand why progressive practices work well in this situation. Through creative, personalized methods, you are capitalizing on the manifest needs and interests of your students to motivate them to learn.		Straying from the essentials of the basic curriculum is often done at the expense of order, discipline, and good achievement test scores. Be wary of this and be sure that you are clear as to what is essential in the curriculum to teach.

Case 5.11: Principal Asks You to Demonstrate Good Teaching for Fellow Teacher

You are a teacher with 2 years' experience and no tenure. Another teacher is new in the school and teaches the same grade level as you do. The teacher is having extreme difficulty in organizing for instruction. These difficulties don't seem to bother the teacher, but the principal is very concerned. The principal calls you in and asks, "Would you consider taking over the problem teacher's classes for a couple of days while the teacher observes you? Let me know as soon as you can if you will help me on this matter."

What will your reaction be? Please choose from the following responses:

1. Take over the problem teacher's class for a couple of days and demonstrate your best teaching.
2. Use all of your public relations skills and convince the principal that it would be unwise to move ahead with the principal's plan.
3. Propose an alternative to the principal. Have the problem teacher into your classroom on occasion and/or teach together when desirable.
4. Tell the problem teacher that the principal is worried about the teacher's instruction.

Case 5.11: Rationales for the Alternative Responses

1. The teacher will be able to see in concrete terms what needs to be done to be a good teacher. Unfortunately, the message is: "I'm okay. You're not okay." Seek a better response.
2. The principal's plan is flawed and simply will create more problems than it is worth. Therefore, talk him out of it. The principal is expected to play an authoritative role when action needs to be taken. Therefore, choose a better response.

3. This is probably the best response. It is more informal and potentially less threatening. It should give the problem teacher the feeling that a team of teachers can make a difference.
4. This gets the message across in very clear terms. The teacher is a problem and should hear this directly. This response can be destructive to the teacher's confidence and self-esteem. It also places you in the roles of conduit and evaluator, not roles that have been assigned to you at school. Choose a better response.

Case 5.12: Personality Conflict With Principal

You are teaching in a school where the principal and you have a personality conflict. In addition, you begin to feel that your professional qualities are being overlooked. For example, you get no praise for a job well done and you are not recommended for special workshops you applied for at various times.

What is your response? Please choose from the following responses:

1. Talk to other teachers about this problem.
2. Talk to your principal's supervisor in the central office—probably one of the assistant superintendents.
3. Talk to the principal and see if there are ways in which you can clear the air and understand each other better.
4. Just go about your business and do the best you can without talking to others about the problem.

Case 5.12: Rationales for the Alternative Responses

1. This will make you feel less lonely and probably will give you emotional support. You can get the matter off your chest. But usually, each person tells at least one other person. It is likely the principal will hear that you are talking about him. Seek a better response.

2. Going over someone's head often gets results fast. The difficulty is that the principal will probably be very angry you took that course of action. Try another response.
3. This is probably the best response. It is direct, and you can give the principal straight signals. The principal may disagree with you, but can't fault you for being deceitful.
4. This approach has the advantage of others not knowing and saying that you have gone behind the principal's back. Unfortunately, it can be a very lonely solution to a matter that needs attention. Seek a better response.

Case 5.13: Superintendent Disrupts Your Teaching Plans to Hear a Consultant Friend

Your superintendent of schools has a number of informal and formal political skills that have brought funds to the school system. The superintendent has a network of educator friends who exchange favors from time to time.

At noon on Wednesday, during the second week of school, the principal of your school announces that students will be released an hour early so that the faculty and staff can assemble in the cafeteria to hear a speech given by a national expert on creativity. You have planned an exciting lesson for this hour and find the last-minute change of plans disruptive.

You attend the lecture, which is given by a speaker who has had no experience as a teacher in public schools. The lecture is highly theoretical, and teachers wonder how in the world this last-minute presentation was arranged and why. The grapevine provides the answer. The speaker is an old friend of the superintendent from the university where the superintendent got a doctorate. Having the speaker lecture to a captive audience was a way the superintendent could return a favor to the visiting professor. Furthermore, you learn that the lecturer was paid $1,000 for the hour lecture.

What is your response? Please choose the best response from the alternatives that follow:

1. Recognize that this is par for the course and do nothing.
2. Talk to your principal in a very direct and honest manner so that your principal knows your views on this matter.
3. Write to your superintendent or talk to your superintendent, making your views on this matter known in an honest way.
4. Take your views to the faculty advisory council.
5. Use your informal communication network with teachers in the school and school system to make your views known.

Case 5.13: Rationales for the Alternative Responses

1. Political forces will always control school systems because they are organized top-down. Commands from above are given, and compliance from below is expected. It is simply a waste of resources to fight this "system." However, this position perpetuates corruption. Find a better response.
2. You will feel better having expressed your views, and the principal will know you have values and take stands. The principal has achieved a level of political expertise and can use this knowledge to assess the situation, and act if it is wise to do so. The difficulty with this response is that the principal is a member of the "administrative club" and will probably find it necessary to support club members rather than you. Seek a better response.
3. This is an honest, direct response that will not send mixed signals. You can be faulted for your position, but you will not be considered deceitful. The difficulty with this approach is that a superintendent who acts this way will probably be the kind of person who is thoroughly entrenched in questionable behavior, and you and your school could be punished for your behavior. Consider other responses.
4. This is probably the best response. You will sense your efficacy and increase your self-esteem by taking action through professional channels. After all, the faculty advisory council was created for teachers to voice their views. There is safety in numbers. If action is taken, others will have to respond to the council.

5. You will feel better having vented your views. If you do this in a sophisticated way, it will be difficult to trace the source. However, you will probably pay a price internally, if not from others, by not being more direct. Find a better response.

Case 5.14: Controversy Over Teachers' Meeting

You have just attended another faculty meeting where insignificant issues were the order of the day. You feel that really important matters were left unsolved, and time was spent on petty issues. Most faculty meetings have been like this under the new principal.

What do you do? Please choose from the following responses:

1. Discuss this meeting with others to get their opinions, then have those who feel as you do approach the principal as a group.
2. Wait until the next meeting and then voice your opinion.
3. Talk to the principal privately and ask what can be done in the future concerning the meetings. Volunteer to help the principal if this help is wanted.
4. Take the matter to the faculty advisory council.

Case 5.14: Rationales for the Alternative Responses

1. You will feel better in talking to others so that your views are known. The difficulty is that such talk may be seen as gossiping, and going as a group can be seen as ganging up on the principal. Seek a better response.
2. This will also give you a sense of efficacy (making a difference) in front of your colleagues. But it is difficult for the principal to save face in this formal setting. You are almost certain to alienate the principal with this approach and therefore lose any real influence you might have.
3. This is the best response. You will give straightforward advice in a one-to-one setting where the principal can save face. Your volunteering to help demonstrates that you are

willing to give resources to this challenge, instead of simply being a critic.
4. This is also a good response because you are taking action in a professional forum. However, you will not be talking to the principal first, which is a courtesy. Try another response.

Case 5.15: An Administrator Asks Teachers for Help on the School Bond Issue

The principal was most interested in demonstrating to his superiors that he was behind their efforts to pass a school bond election. The principal, therefore, asked his teachers to do everything possible to support the passing of the issue at hand. Some teachers argued that teachers are professionals and therefore should not take part in this kind of political issue. They said that the teacher should be somewhat detached from the students and parents in relating to this matter. They added that teachers are not interested in the mechanics of getting money, and therefore the administration should deal with this matter. Another group of teachers felt that the teachers should take an active part in the matter and even go from door to door to sell the public on the school bond issue. You are a teacher in the school.

What will you do? Please choose the best of the following alternative responses:

1. Keep your opinion to yourself and go about your business, not talking to colleagues.
2. Make your views known to your colleagues and try to get them to unite in favor of your position.
3. Work through your teachers' organization to get the bond issue passed.
4. Go directly to the principal and let the principal know how you feel on this matter.
5. Speak to your students on the issue involved.

Case 5.15: Rationales for the Alternative Responses

1. A low profile does not make waves. You simply will not be involved, thus saving your resources of time, energy, and expertise. However, you sense that you are not exercising your power in any way. Seek another response.
2. A high political profile will earn the respect of some colleagues, who will see you as a risk taker. You will feel you are "on the team." But this high profile can also get you into a lot of trouble. Consider a better response.
3. This response will also give you a team feeling. However, unlike with the previous response, you will have the formal machinery of the teachers' organization behind you; whereas, with the previous response, you could be left out on a limb by yourself. This is probably the best response.
4. This affords the advantage of sharing straight signals with your principal and acting as a safety valve for the release of your feelings. But action will probably stop at this point. Therefore, consider a better response.
5. This will provide for active students in an active classroom and it will give you the good feeling of venting your ideas and opinions. However, using your students for political purposes can get you into a lot of trouble with administrators and parents. Therefore, consider a better response.

Case 5.16: Administrator Pressures New Teacher to Join Teacher Organization

You are a first-year teacher, and your administrative superior also happens to be the building representative for the combined local-state-national educational associations. He personally encourages you to join these associations. However, you have not decided whether to join the education associations or the local teachers' union. When you mention this, he says that the union members are just troublemakers and that you should stay away from them for your own good. When you don't immediately join, he makes a plea at faculty meeting for 100% membership in the education associations. Since you are the only new teacher, and the school has apparently had 100% membership in the past, the point of his remarks is not lost on anyone.

How will you respond? Choose from these alternative responses:

1. Join the local-state-national organizations to avoid conflict with the administrator.
2. Join the teachers' union and ask for protection from the administrator.
3. Do not join any organization, but contact the teachers' union about administrative pressure.
4. Do not join any organization and hope to maintain a neutral position.
5. Announce that you will take your time to determine the benefits of the professional associations, as well as those of the union, before making any decision to join.
6. See the superintendent and register a complaint about pressure from the administrator.

Case 5.16: Rationales for the Alternative Responses

1. As a first-year teacher, you do not want to fail to do something that will enhance your chances of achieving career status or tenure after your probationary period is over. You understand that you will need a favorable evaluation from this administrator to gain tenure, so you decide not to alienate him on this matter that is apparently so important to him. You join the professional associations. Perhaps they are the best choice after all, since the school has apparently had 100% membership in the past. On the other hand, this course of action is not a courageous stand. Please select a different response.
2. Since the teachers' union is the only competitor for the educational associations, it will have a vested interest in protecting its members from administrative harassment. Pressure, in the form of monitoring from the union lead-

ership, will force the administrator to evaluate your performance in an equitable, professional manner. The administrator will understand that a grievance will likely be filed if you are punished in any way because of your choice in the matter of professional membership. After all, such matters are extraneous to the evaluation of one's performance. This course of action offers protection, but perhaps leads to affiliation for the wrong reasons. Please choose another course of action.

3. By making this choice, you gain the advocacy and protection of the union from administrative harassment, without actually affiliating with the union. Union pressure will probably force the administrator to evaluate your performance in an equitable and professional manner. The administrator may feel, however, that by not choosing to join the union, you might still be led to join the educational associations in the future. The problem with this response is that you benefit from the union's protection without contributing to it in any way. There is a better answer. Please try again.

4. By making it known that you will not join any organization but remain neutral on the matter, you establish your independence. Perhaps this is a safe strategy during the years you are a probationary teacher. Certainly, the administrator would not view this stance as defiant by establishing some type of association with the union that he opposes. The problem with this stance is that you forego any potential benefits of professional membership. Please choose another course of action.

5. This is the best response. In this way you establish your independence in a manner that is legitimate. You don't rush into any decision. You wish to focus on what is good about each option, not negative stereotypes. The union and the professional associations will continue to pursue your allegiance, but will not be in a position to say that you are benefiting from their actions without paying the cost of membership. After all, they don't want to alienate you. The administrator probably will not be alienated by

your stance, because it seems so reasonable. You will un-
doubtedly get through some administrative evaluations
that are not biased. After a lengthy period of inquiry, you
can make an informed choice about which organization best
suits your long-term personal and professional interests.

6. The superintendent is your building administrator's superior. In that position, he might or might not offer you some
degree of protection from your administrator's bias against
the teachers' union. There would be an official record of
your concern. Perhaps your building administrator would
be influenced by your assertiveness in the face of his overt
pressure. On the other hand, you might alienate your administrator more by going over his head. Choose a less
risky course of action.

6 PARENT–TEACHER CONFLICT

"Sources of conflict" between parents and teachers refers to differences in perceptions parents and teachers have as to what schools should do, what schools presently do, and what schools can do. The perception of conflict adds to a conflict situation, or creates one where it did not in fact previously exist. In the latter case, for example, a rumor, although completely unfounded, creates tension when known to the party(ies) involved in the rumor. A conflict situation is thus created. Such situations often involve parents and teachers.

To understand our schools we must turn then to the perceptions of parents and teachers in the school as a social system. The study of conflict and conflict situations is consistent with the case method employed in this book. Although schools involve more than conflicts, conflict resolution is a major part of the operation of schools, and this resolution includes teachers and parents.

Teachers Not Trusted

The mass media have a tremendous influence on parents' perceptions of schools in general. Gallup polls in the present decade demonstrate that more than half of the public surveyed graded schools in general as C, D, or F (Elam, Rose, & Gallup, 1991, 1992). At the same time, there is a substantial disparity between the grades people give their local schools and the grades people give schools in our nation. That is, a halo effect exists, with the public grading their local schools at least 20% higher, in the A and B categories, than schools nationally (Elam et al., 1991). However, even local schools were graded their lowest by the public in 1983, when a Gallup poll was taken shortly after the appearance of *A Nation at Risk,* a report in book form that criticized American schools in contrast to Japanese schools (Elam et al., 1991).

The most plausible explanation for the halo effect is that "the more firsthand knowledge one has about the public schools, the more favorable one's perception of them." Or stated another way, "familiarity with the public schools breeds respect" (Elam et al., 1991, p. 54). It is important to note, however, that public high school teachers "in this community" are graded A and B about 15% less than are elementary school teachers "in this community" (Elam et al., 1991, p. 54).

Who are the most dissatisfied groups in their evaluation of American schools, groups that favor radical changes in them? They are blacks and inner-city dwellers, groups that obviously overlap considerably. A major element in their criticism is low quality of teachers. How do we explain this lack of trust? Mary M. Kennedy, director of Michigan State University's National Center for Research on Teacher Learning, speaks to this question:

Teachers' backgrounds are often also limited with respect to the kinds of people they have encountered. Most teachers come from small, homogeneous, lower middle-class communities. They attend college in nearby communities and hope to return to their home town or to a neighboring town to teach. Their exposure to students who are even marginally different from themselves is often close to nonexistent (Kennedy, 1991, p. 7).

At the same time, these place-bound teachers "may have never encountered wealthy or socially ambitious students" (Kennedy, 1991, p. 7). The result is that many teachers are persons in the middle who don't connect with those in social strata above or below them. Due to changing demographics, the problem is likely to be accentuated rather than diminished. For example, during the present decade it is predicted that "five million children of immigrants will be entering the K-12 school systems" (Michigan Education Association, 1992, p. 13). At present, "more than 150 languages are represented in schools nationwide and nearly that many in some large school systems" (Michigan Education Association, 1992, p. 13). If we add to this more single-parent families and an increasing number of families in which both parents work, we can see how these changing forces will drive American education and schools (Michigan Education Association, 1992).

A diminishing trust in teachers is evidenced by an increase in teacher-bashing. Teacher-bashing in the media is followed by a clarion call for the best and brightest to go into teaching as a profession. Demoralized by this contradiction, prospective and present teachers feel a lack of trust. It is also difficult for teachers to consider themselves as professionals when they are not trusted to deal with controversial issues in the classroom. Special interest groups are a reality in today's society, a society in which people want participatory democracy rather than simply a representative democracy. Teachers often feel like persons in the middle, who may or may not be supported by their administrators when there is "heat in the kitchen." How do teachers react to the feeling that they are not trusted? Some teachers simply leave the profession, whereas others move into administrative positions for higher pay and more positional authority. Others go to graduate school in pursuit of positions in higher education. Those who stay in teaching may find the lack of trust demoralizing at times, but find ways to deal with the situation. The main payoff for teachers in such situations is the feeling that they are making a difference in the lives of their students. Many teachers recognize their own political efficacy and, armed with information on the reality of the situation, do what they can as creative leaders in their school and the school system as a whole. To deny the reality of the situation described in the following passage is to deny one's power to make a difference as a teacher:

> Teachers commonly suffer from low self-esteem and poor perceptions by the public. These are results of misinterpretations of simplistic data such as average SAT scores and invalid international comparisons. "This unfortunate cycle of low self-esteem followed by unfounded criticism from the public raises the specter of a downward spiral in future education quality," concludes the summary of the Sandia study (Michigan Education Association, 1992, p. 13).

Parents Have Unrealistic Expectations for Their Children

Another source of conflict between teachers and parents is parents who have unrealistic expectations for their children. An example is school discipline. Discipline, along with drug use and lack of school funding, "are virtually tied as the most frequently mentioned problem with which the local public schools must deal" (Elam et al., 1991, p. 55).

The difficulty is that some parents expect teachers to discipline their children in a way that they are not disciplined at home (Waller, 1965). It is easier in many cases for a parent to give the child money and possessions, rather than the time and energy that are required to create and sustain a disciplinary structure.

Many parents, especially in suburbia, push their children beyond their capacities. Parents want their children to read by the time they are in kindergarten, be loved by the opposite sex at age 7, and begin their higher education at 17—in a prestigious university, if possible. One humorist has suggested that children be given a B.A. at birth, an M.A. at age 2, a Ph.D. at 5, and then let the schools get on with the child's learning. The union card to higher education is a record of good grades. Little wonder that parents pressure teachers for such grades, thus revealing a most important source of conflict between parents and teachers. The student returns home with a poor report card, and the parents have to rationalize this in some way. Frequently, the teacher receives the brunt of the criticism. The teacher does not know how to teach, it is claimed, because the student received a poor grade, or the teacher had a personality conflict with the student.

At the same time, it should be added that some parents are uninterested in schools. Such apathy is often the result of their own dislike for school when they were students. The result is that the teachers do not feel that they are getting the kind of support they deserve from the parents. The child, in turn, does not receive support at home for accomplishments at school.

It is difficult for many parents to accept their children's limitations, for these are a reflection of the parents' influence on the child. Yet it is also true that many of the child's limitations are the result, in part, of the school's failures. The student who is decidedly different from the majority of the students is difficult to deal with, for the teacher is pressured to deal with the majority of the students. Such a student often manifests undesirable behavior patterns. The teacher then frequently becomes overwhelmed with specific behavior problems, which hinder developing the latent ability of each student. For example, maturation differences in boys and girls are great at different levels of their school careers. Yet, it is difficult for teachers to take this important variable into account, given the large number of students they teach and the intensity of classroom interaction.

Parents' Double Standard

There is evidence that parents expect the schools to teach their children desirable manners and morals. In most states, these values are supported by law. California law traditionally read as follows: "Each teacher shall endeavor to impress upon the minds of the pupils the principles of morality, truth, justice, patriotism, and a true comprehension of the rights, duties, and dignity of American citizenship, to teach them to avoid idleness, profanity, and falsehood, and to instruct them in manners and morals and the principles of a free government" (*Education Code*, 1963, p. 356).

At the same time that there is support for prescriptions such as the above, some parents sign letters claiming illness for their children when they skip school. Other parents want the schools to train their children to work diligently, but they do their children's homework. Double standards on the part of parents are an important source of friction between teachers and parents.

Parents Afraid of Innovation

Parents become accustomed to certain behavior on the part of teachers, and when this tradition is broken by innovation, parents become anxious. A communication problem and lack of understanding exist. The modern movement to the whole language approach in reading programs serves as a case in point. Social change must always be made legitimate in the minds of parents if the change is to be successful. This frequently occurs after the parents live with the change for some time and see that their child benefits.

Homework and Discipline

Homework is tangible evidence of student progress. The parents know via homework that *something* academic is going on in the school. Homework is, however, a double-edged sword for the teacher. If parents judge homework to be busywork, or irrelevant, or inappropriate, the teacher is considered incompetent. Homework is also visible evidence of the teacher's desire to discipline the minds of the students.

Some parents complain because the school does not discipline their students enough; others complain because the school does discipline the students—usually their child has been punished, thus causing the parents to rush to the child's support. Some parents object to dress standards. The school is damned if it does and damned if it doesn't.

Conclusion

Parents and teachers vie for the support of the student. Some parents are threatened because a teacher commands more respect from their child than they do. Part of this is due to hero worship, which exists at specific times in a child's life, but such respect is also due to the fact that many parents have made significant mistakes in raising their children—mistakes they cannot easily admit.

Parents often use their children as pawns for their own prestige in the community and with friends. Some parents constantly compare their children with other children they know. The child who competes favorably usually does not object to this practice; the child who does not compete favorably, however, often becomes alienated from his parents and the school. The result is discord between the parents and the child's teacher.

Case 6.1: Parent Contradicts Self in Speech to Faculty

The principal has appointed you as chair of the staff development committee. The parent of one of your students is a promi-
nent businessman in your community and a dynamic speaker.
You have invited him to speak to the faculty at the beginning of
the year on the subject "A Parent's View of School Reform."

The speaker begins with a brief sketch of his life, from its
origins on a farm to his present position of prominence in his
region of the country. He outlines the secret to success in general
and his success in particular: (a) the ability to hustle—set goals
and go after them; (b) perseverance; (c) people skills; and (d)
excellent follow-through. He speaks with passion about how he
graduated from the "school of hard knocks," with his ability to
draw from his many and diverse experiences as the main key to
his success.

Then he moves to a critique of the schools. He argues that
schools have neglected the basics of reading, writing, and mathematics. He elaborates by saying that schools should get rid of the
frills and give attention only to the basic subjects.

Later in the day your principal asks for your views on the
speaker's presentation. What will you say?

(extreme response) Progressive	neutral	(extreme response) Essentialist
The first part of the speaker's address is correct. People skills, hard work, setting goals, and follow-through arc the keys to success in life; but they are not what much of curriculum and instruction in schools emphasize. Standard curriculum as a course of study is aimed at covering material (textbooks), usually at the expense of critical thinking. The speaker's solution of returning to the basics contradicts his earlier remarks. Basic instruction emphasizes product (i.e., content) rather than process (such as goal setting). This contradiction must be clearly spelled out as you state your views to the principal. You should add that many self-made business people fail to see this contradiction.		The bottom line is that the speaker supports the essentialist position that we have neglected the basics of reading, writing, and mathematics. The curriculum has been taken over by frills and fads. There is somewhat of a contradiction in the speaker's statements, but this is typical of many self-made men of his era. The contradiction is minor and of little consequence.

Case 6.2: Parent Group Wants Special Attention Given to African-American Heritage

A vocal group of African-American parents asks for and receives time to speak to the faculty at your school. They argue forcefully that teachers need to give more attention to African-American heritage. Furthermore, they are very specific in their request that the curriculum be changed to make more room for African-American studies. They add that the present curriculum has a heavy bias toward European culture, with such African studies as art, music, and literature largely neglected.

As a faculty member, what is your reaction?

(extreme response) Progressive	neutral	(extreme response) Essentialist
History and circumstances change. This is a basic tenet of progressivism. The curriculum must reflect these basic changes. There has been a heavy bias in favor of European culture at the expense of Africa and Asia. Traditional curriculum does not meet "the public test." That is, it has not kept up with the fact that the United States of America has increasingly become a nation of color. We must have curriculum content and materials that emphasize learning through living with today's realities. There are emerging bodies of knowledge, not a single traditional body of knowledge. Support the proposal.		Traditional knowledge has withstood the test of time. Not only is some knowledge more valuable than other knowledge, but this knowledge is also essential to achieving good scores on standardized achievement tests and the Scholastic Aptitude Test. Many courses, such as the one proposed, are in fact anti-intellectual. Therefore, reject the proposal.

Case 6.3: Some Parents Fight to Keep Tracking

After reviewing relevant research and consulting within the field, the new superintendent of schools worked with her staff to design a plan to move the schools away from their system of tracking students. Opposition to this plan began to surface when the school board held hearings on the subject. This opposition was primarily located in the upper-middle-class neighborhoods in general, and the country club area in particular. The bottom line for these parents is that they want their children to be in classes with "the nice people"—that is, people like themselves.

You have been appointed to a committee of K-12 teachers in your system, whose members serve to advise the superintendent on this matter.

What will your advice be?

(extreme response) Progressive	neutral	(extreme response) Essentialist
Tracking is anti-democratic: The rich get richer and the poor get poorer. Those who support tracking want a special advantage for their children. In effect, they want their children to only spend time with "the nice people" (people like themselves). Progressives, in fact, are opposed to any type of ability grouping or any type of segregation of students of the same chronological age, whether it is done on the basis of sex, race, social class, or academic performance. Advise the superintendent to oppose tracking and support your superintendent as she fights tracking.		Ability grouping keeps the gifted student from being cheated by accommodating individual differences and scholastic aptitude. Ability grouping is of great importance in English, mathematics, science, and languages. It is not necessary in the less academically rigorous subjects. Support the upper-middle-class parents who lead the opposition to the superintendent.

Case 6.4: Parent Volunteer Reports Testing Irregularities

You are a respected teacher in a medium-size school system. You have received a letter from a parent volunteer who spends a good deal of time in an elementary school. The letter contains the following comments:

> There has been a good deal of coverage of testing irregu-larities (cheating) on television (such as "60 Minutes") and in newspapers.
>
> Since I love my job as a parent volunteer, I must remain anonymous and trust you to assure this. How-ever, I have been an actual witness to these things as teachers have given the C.A.T. (California Achievement Test):
>
> 1. Stopping mid-test to teach something coming up on the test that the students had not been taught;
> 2. Before handing in the tests given that day, looking ahead to copy down the upcoming test questions and teaching them verbatim;
> 3. Tapping a child on the shoulder to point out an incorrect answer and giving him the A-OK sign when he erased it and filled in the correct answer;
> 4. Going overtime;
> 5. Allowing children to go back and finish up pre-vious sections that they had not completed within the time limit;
> 6. Reading the directions more than once to the chil-dren or paraphrasing them to emphasize what the teacher especially wanted the children to know; and
> 7. Allowing the children to have little math-fact cheat cards in their desks that they could refer to during the test, since they never learned math facts on their own.

What will you do, if anything?

(extreme response) Progressive	neutral	(extreme response) Essentialist
Cheating cannot be condoned but must be put in the context of modern society. The essentialists' unrelenting emphasis on high achievement test scores has reached epidemic proportions, with cheating the natural result. It should not be surprising that the teacher observed by the parent volunteer is guilty of the testing irregularities reported in the letter. Share the letter with your principal in confidence, but be sure to provide the context discussed above.		The point is that cheating simply cannot be tolerated, because it is not only wrong but also contaminates test score results of students who have done well on tests without cheating. Report this matter to your principal and director of testing. Insist that the matter be thoroughly investigated and that appropriate action be taken, including the retesting of the classes involved and appropriate punishment of the culpable teachers. Anyone who trashes the academic process must be punished.

Case 6.5: PTA Speaker Endorses National Curriculum Standards

The president of your school's Parent Teacher Association is a professor from a nearby university. The PTA president has invited a nationally recognized education expert to speak at the fall meeting. You are invited to respond to the speaker's address because you are the head of the faculty advisory council.

A large turnout is present for the address, and the speaker delivers a dynamic and often humorous lecture. She argues that national education policy has been set for the next 4 to 8 years, and at the head of the list is the need for national education standards, national curriculum frameworks, and a national examination system. She adds that the national examinations will tell us how curriculum is operationally defined. Evaluation of students will include performance assessment, projects, and portfolios. The speaker concludes by saying that we will have to live with a paradox: a national orientation to education that is local in implementation. And teachers must serve as coaches who will help students beat Educational Testing Service in much the same way that Advanced Placement teachers presently try to beat the test makers. Teachers who are up to it will be inventive brokers who relate to the national-local paradox. Such teachers will do extraordinary work to reach and surpass national standards. Competition will be the driving force that will elicit the best in teachers and students. When the system is working correctly, it will look much like architectural competition. All competitors must meet building codes, but creativity will bloom.

It is now time for you to speak. What will you say?

(extreme response) Progressive	neutral	(extreme response) Essentialist
The idea of a national curriculum with a national examination system is a serious mistake that runs counter to the tenets of progressivism. Each child is unique and should be challenged to use his or her talents to the best of his or her ability. The speaker's position, if implemented, would sort students into winners and losers. It is an anti-democratic position. You must argue against the speaker's position in a forceful manner.		The speaker is on target. We must have high expectations for all children. We have made education so unresponsive to the individual that we have neglected standards. In fact, the speaker's position is very democratic because it is a pathway to equal opportunity for all who will work hard. Therefore, a democracy based on merit can finally be achieved in our country. All children will benefit. Support the speaker's position in a forceful manner.

Case 6.6: A Colleague Responds to a Parent at an Open House

You are a member of a teaching team that includes math, science, social studies, and English. It is open house early in the fall, and parents are walking an abbreviated form of the schedule followed by their children.

You are in a room with the math teacher when a bright, articulate parent asks, "Can you tell me if this math course will be useful to my child in other math courses to be taken, and also in college?" The math teacher responds, "I really have no earthly idea."

What will you do?

(extreme response) Progressive	neutral	(extreme response) Essentialist
The teacher is not at fault. The teacher education program that the teacher attended probably didn't give the teacher practice in explaining what he or she is going to do or has done and why. The principal of the school is also probably at fault for not giving staff development experiences that provide teachers with practice in explaining teaching actions. Because the progressive individualizes instruction and uses a variety of teaching approaches, it is		You have just witnessed the reason why progressivism is misdirected, and essentialism is correct. The essentialist not only emphasizes the basics but is clear as to the linear, sequential order in which essential knowledge is covered. You must use your leadership ability on the teaching team to move team members into the essentialist camp, so that they can offer clear, time-tested, no-nonsense explanations of what they are doing and why.

(continued)

(extreme response) Progressive	neutral	(extreme response) Essentialist

very important that teachers learn how to articulate what they do and why. Use your leadership ability as a team member to influence the principal and central office leaders to provide staff development experiences that will help teachers learn to explain what they do and why. Videotaping, role playing, and simulation games are especially helpful in such staff development matters.

In conclusion, as progressives, we don't purport to guarantee learning outcomes the way essentialists do. Rather, we facilitate learning outcomes. What is gained is in large measure due to the individual student's initiative and effort. This must be understood in light of the fact that some critics will say that the teacher's response is outrageous and surly.

Case 6.7: Potential Conflict About Religion With Critical Parents

Robert is a secondary-school student from a religiously conservative family. He is a good student who is somewhat removed from other students in his grade. He is a devoted member of a local church, whose youth group meets each Wednesday morning for a prayer service.

Robert's mother and father, who is presently out of work, have been critical of your teaching. They have taken their criticism to the principal, who has supported your teaching.

Just before your first period class on Wednesday, Robert's best friend comes to you with the following story: "This morning at prayer meeting Robert started praying in front of the whole group and his prayer was a mixture of our church's ideas and the ideas you have been teaching about world religions. It really sounded strange. He repeated everything he learned in the lesson on Zen Buddhism."

What will you do?

(extreme response) Progressive	neutral	(extreme response) Essentialist
This is the kind of challenge a creative, innovative teacher faces. You avoid such controversy if you use a "paint by the numbers" approach to the curriculum. But you and the students suffer from such a stifling teaching methodology. Talk to like-minded teachers who will support you as you continue to teach in a creative manner. Talk to the principal about the value of your		Once again, we see the downside of liberal progressivism. Zen Buddhism has no place in the curriculum. It simply is not essential knowledge and should have never been taught. You must get the curriculum back on track, rather than teaching frills that happen to interest you. If you wish, talk to the principal in order to cover your bases, but inform the principal that you will

(continued)   *(continued)*

(extreme response) Progressive	neutral	(extreme response) Essentialist
teaching methodology so that the principal is informed and aware of your ability to explain what you are doing and why—the hallmark of a professional educator. In conclusion, you cannot be held responsible or accountable for what an individual student does with newly acquired knowledge. After all, you have encouraged him to think independently. Also, with regard to Zen Buddhism and other "foreign" ideas, teaching about something should not be confused with advocacy of that thing. In short, you were not proselytizing.		give leadership to implementing the essentialist position. Also, use your leadership ability to convince colleagues to move to the essentialist camp. That will help focus the curriculum on basic knowledge or content that the general public understands and supports.

Case 6.8: Influential Parent Attempts to Persuade You to Change His Son's Grade

You are a teacher in a suburban high school. You feel that the performance of the students in your class is poor and you give the majority of the class C, D, and F grades in spite of the fact that the class is considered college preparatory. The father of one of your students, to whom you gave a D grade for the semester, comes to discuss his child's progress and the grades given in your class. He is very concerned about the low semester grade and does not believe his child deserved to get such a low grade. He suggests to you that you should be more flexible in your evaluation of students and you should change his child's grade to at least a C, so that his child's chances of getting into a good college will not be ruined. He makes a point of stressing the fact that his child is a hard worker but not a quick learner, a point that you openly agree is true. At the end of the conference, the father mentions that he is an established, influential member of the community and has friends on the Board of Education. What will your reaction be?

(extreme response) Progressive	neutral	(extreme response) Essentialist
The father's attempt to use his influence in a political way is bothersome, but should not detract from a good point that emerged during your conversation with the father; namely, his child did work very hard during the semester but simply was not a quick learner. Review the student's work and change the grade to C if there is evidence to give the student the benefit of the doubt due to effort put forth. Progressives will always weigh legitimate mitigative factors in student evaluation. Do not concern yourself about the appearance of being swayed by political pressure if there are legitimate reasons for changing the grade.		The intellectual growth of the student, as evidenced by grades on papers and tests, is the only criterion to be considered in grading. You may wish to review the student's work to be sure that the semester grade reflects the student's acquisition of essential knowledge. If the student's grades do not average above a D, so be it. You have simply done the correct thing. Do not be swayed by political pressure. You may wish to show an averaging of the student's grades to the principal.

Case 6.9: You Are Asked for Your Definition of Curriculum at a Staff Development Retreat

You are a member of the Site-Based Management Curriculum Council in your school. This five-member group, consisting of three teachers, a parent, and the assistant principal, has planned an excellent conference (retreat) for faculty and five parents who represent the community. You look forward to the good fellowship, food, and recreation.

The opening session consists of a guest speaker from the university, after which there will be five "breakout" groups that will react to the speaker's address. You and the other members of the curriculum council will give leadership to the "breakout" groups.

The speaker challenges the audience to define *curriculum* as what each person experiences as learning settings are cooperatively created, rather than as a course of study. The speaker adds that curriculum as a course of study should be the best it can be, but it is ultimately only a springboard for all of the learning experiences students and teachers acquire.

As the head of one of the five discussion groups, it is your responsibility to begin the discussion by giving your reaction to the speaker. What will you say?

(extreme response) Progressive	neutral	(extreme response) Essentialist
The speaker has delivered a powerful and accurate message. Each person's experiences are central to the curriculum. This includes teachers as well as students. Curriculum as a course of study is indeed only a springboard that must be revised to meet new societal and school needs. Applaud the speaker's message and support it in the discussion group. Also lead the discussion in the direction of how the speaker's message can be applied in the school and classrooms. The curriculum council will have an important role to play in reviewing and revising curriculum as a course of study. The assistant principal and principal will also need to understand that they are coordinators rather than directors.		The speaker's message is very troublesome. It provides each teacher the license to go in any direction he or she pleases. It ignores the fact that there is an essential body of knowledge that must be learned by all students. Raise these points in the discussion group and make it clear that the school would be in chaos if the speaker's views were implemented. For one thing, teachers could not assume that important prerequisite content had been covered and mastered.

Case 6.10: Parent Pressures Principal to Change Student's Grade

Your school draws students from some housing areas that are highly college-oriented, and there is a status difference in the community, based on the college or university one's children attend. Because of the pressure from an angry parent who is quite influential in the community, a student's semester grade has been changed by the principal from a D to a C. As this student's teacher, you know that the student deserved a D and certainly never deserved a C. You also believe that a hardworking student from a less-advantaged part of town would not have been given this favored treatment.

What will you do? Please choose from the following alternatives:

1. Simply ignore the matter because there is nothing you can really do. The principal has the legal or official right to change grades.
2. Talk with the parents of the student, perhaps with the school counselor present, and try to help them see the ramifications of what they are doing.
3. Talk with the student person-to-person so that the student understands the ramifications of what has been done.
4. Have class discussions about what a real education means.
5. Meet with the principal who changed the grade and state your case. If the principal's response is not satisfactory, state to the principal that you will appeal the matter to a higher administrative authority.

Case 6.10: Rationales for the Alternative Responses

1. It is true that the principal is officially responsible for matters in the school and can change grades. It would be a waste of your resources to fight the system. However, you probably won't feel very good about yourself and your lack of initiative in dealing with the matter. Search for a better response.

2. This response has the advantage of your taking action on behalf of your views. The counselor could lend support and is trained to deal with difficult matters like this. The disadvantage of this approach is that you are not directing the matter to the person or persons in the administration who overturned the grade. Consider other responses.

3. The student is certainly in on the parent's request for a grade change. A person-to-person discussion with the student could give you information as to what is going on in the parent's mind and why. It is a disadvantage of this approach, however, that other parties to the controversy are excluded. Look for a better response.

4. Class discussions could lead one or more students to consider what education is all about. Good behavior could be reinforced, and inappropriate behavior could be changed. But this is a private matter at the moment between you and the principal who changed the grade. Class discussions could leave others with the feeling that you are an alarmist and unprofessional. Consider other responses.

5. This is the best response for this particular time. By meeting with the principal who changed the grade, you will not be criticized for going behind his or her back. After talking to the principal, you are still in a position to escalate this matter by going over his or her head. However, you will inform the principal who changed the grade of your intentions and therefore not be deceitful.

Case 6.11: Parent Accuses You of Picking on Child

You call the parents of a student in your class to schedule a conference. The student has been doing poor work, has a poor attitude toward school, but has good ability. Only one of the parents attends the conference, and when you summarize the student's progress, the parent says, "You are picking on my child." (The child is not present at the conference.)

What is your response? Please choose from the following alternatives:

1. Simply ignore what the parent has said, continue with any unfinished business, and bring the conference to a close.
2. Confront the parent and point out that such "victim talk" on a parent's part can be a major part of a child's problem.
3. Say that you do not think you have picked on the child, but will check yourself in the future to be sure your perceptions are accurate and make adjustments accordingly, if necessary. Continue with the conference in a very professional manner and invite the parent back for further discussions.
4. Say that you do not think you are picking on the child, but will call the principal into the room as a third party to hear this case.

Case 6.11: Rationales for the Alternative Responses

1. This is a straightforward approach to this problem and has all of the advantages of this. For example, the parent gets straight signals about your desire not to deal with this matter at the moment. This response also buys time for you to consider what to do next, if anything. This response could well be considered too abrupt by the parent. Therefore, consider other responses.
2. You will bring to the parent's attention the role the parent is playing in this problem situation. The parent may then consider how he or she is adding to or creating the problem. When people are confronted with being victims, they counterattack and there is little if any room for negotiation. Examine other responses.
3. This is probably the best response. You are playing the role of a statesman, willing to examine and possibly change your behavior. Your professional manner will buy you time to consider next steps, if needed.
4. You buy time and have the advantage of hearing the reaction of a third party, one in a position of authority above you. However, the principal may consider it premature to have such a conference and may question your ability to

handle such matters on your own. The principal cannot be bothered about all matters of this nature. Consider other responses.

Case 6.12: Parent Wants Child in Your Class

You have recently been hired as a teacher in your home town. You excitedly share the news of employment with your supportive neighbors, forgetting that they have a daughter entering your teaching grade level this year. You have shared your teaching philosophy with this family in the past, and they have shown much enthusiasm. After you tell them you have been hired to teach, they immediately tell you that they will request their daughter's placement in your class. You appreciate the confidence in your teaching ability but are concerned about the degree of closeness with the parents and the child.

How will you handle this situation? Please choose from the following responses:

1. Talk to the child's parents and say that you do not think it would be a good thing to have their daughter in your class, but you will continue to keep an eye out for her in school.
2. You think that you are able to separate the professional from the personal. Do not worry about having this child in your class. Agree to it.
3. Talk to the principal about this matter. Let the principal be "the bad guy" by not placing the child in your class.
4. Just ignore the matter and let the chips fall where they may. After all, the principal's experienced judgment might lead to the child's being placed with another teacher.

Case 6.12: Rationales for the Alternative Responses

1. This is probably the best response, given your concern about the degree of closeness with the parents and the child. You are a new teacher in the school and will have enough pressure without additional stress.

2. This situation is one of many professional challenges you will deal with as a teacher. You have a fine education and are confident that you can relate well to professional situations of all kinds. The difficulty is that you may not know at this point in your career how this situation can be very stressful. Choose a better response.
3. Principals are paid more to take the flak in situations like this. And they are more experienced in handling stress. The problem is that word will probably get back to the parents that you did not actively support having the child in your class. You will pay the price for being deceitful. Consider other responses.
4. Teachers often take too seriously matters like this and therefore get nervous about being stressed out. Just relax and do your job. It may be hard to do this, given your concern about this matter. Look at other responses.

Case 6.13: Parent Is Incensed Over Punishment

One morning in the restroom, your homeroom student uses the knife section of a small, innocent-looking nail file to cut another girl's finger. The other girl was teasing her. The victim goes straight to the principal's office and reports the incident. Unfortunately, the alleged perpetrator slipped out of homeroom without your permission while you were monitoring the hallway. She was not supposed to be in the bathroom.

After hearing of her daughter's suspension from the principal (and the circumstances surrounding the incident), the mother comes to your room and proceeds to use abusive and profane language to you in front of your students. She blames the entire situation on you because you were not more watchful.

What is your reaction? Please choose from the following alternatives:

1. Listen to the parent and use verbal persuasion to get her out of the building. At the first opportunity, update the principal.

2. Ask a teacher next door to keep an eye on your class and take the parent to the principal's office so that the principal can participate in this encounter.
3. Call the police and formally charge the parent with trespassing and use of profanity.
4. Write a memo to the principal at the end of the day, spelling out in detail what happened from start to finish.

Case 6.13: Rationales for the Alternative Responses

1. The parent does not seem to be physically violent, so you should be able to steer her out of the building with little trouble. You must update the principal on what happened. This is probably the best response for this difficult situation.
2. The principal has already taken action on this case and will want to be involved in the follow-up situation. The parent will also recognize the principal's higher position of authority and probably tone down. The principal may not be in the office, however, and it will be difficult for the teacher next door to watch both classrooms. Try a better response.
3. It is always a good idea to protect yourself and your students if there is any doubt about your safety. However, this seems premature because the parent does not seem physically violent. It would be an overreaction that appeals to another source of authority and leaves the principal out of the loop.
4. A bureaucratic response, such as writing a report in detail, is always a good way to cover yourself. However, stronger action seems to be called for in this situation—action that will not make it appear that you are hiding from getting involved. Please try another response that will place you in a more openly active leadership role.

Case 6.14: Parent Requests Extra Work to Improve Student's Grade

The parent of one of your academically gifted students comes to you shortly after the mid-9-weeks progress report, expressing a concern over a B in science. You have already discussed her child's careless attitude toward his schoolwork. She requests extra credit work in hopes of raising his grade to an A.

What is your response? Choose from the following responses:

1. Deny the request and explain your rationale for doing so to the mother.
2. Say that you will consider the request and give your answer after doing so.
3. Support the request by inviting the student to do extra credit work, with the understanding that this will raise the student's grade.
4. Support the request by inviting the student to do extra credit work, with the understanding that the quality of the work must be of A caliber to raise his grade. In order to be fair, issue this same invitation to all students you teach.

Case 6.14: Rationales for the Alternative Responses

1. The problem is not the amount of work done but the quality of the work. The student's careless attitude toward his schoolwork is the problem. To raise a grade on the basis of additional work simply reinforces the student's carelessness. Search for a better response.
2. This response buys you time to think through the problem. This may be a good idea, but it fails to give the parent and student the benefit of your professional advice at a time when they are most receptive to your answer. Consider other responses.
3. This gives the student a second chance to improve his grade. However, it doesn't address the problem of his carelessness. Choose another response.

4. This is the best response. The student has a second chance, but it is understood that he must be less careless or his efforts will not suffice to raise his grade. Furthermore, all students are extended the same invitation. That makes for an equitable solution even if it does mean more work for you. It will be worth the trouble if students benefit.

Case 6.15: Parents Question Their Child's Grade

The parents of an academically gifted student in a math class are unhappy with his recent grade of C. It seems that their child is very adept at solving problems in his head and does not feel the need to write down any work. Unfortunately, his refusal to show work has also resulted in computational mistakes, lowering his grade. Because you require work to be shown, his parents contend that you are grading him on not following directions, rather than on his understanding of the material.

How will you handle this problem? Choose from the following responses:

1. Explain to the parents exactly what has happened. Tell them that this problem will persist in college if their child does not correct his practices now.
2. Simply change the grade to B.
3. Invite the math specialist from central office to a conference for the parents that includes you.

Case 6.15: Rationales for the Alternative Responses

1. This is probably the best answer. By dealing directly with the problem and involving the parents, you will have the opportunity to state your views in a clear and concise manner. Because these parents value their child's success in college, they will likely want to do what will best prepare their child for college. You will have made it clear that your primary concern is for their child.
2. This is the most efficient and easiest response. The lesson taught, however, is that you will yield to pressure—

a lesson that will reinforce the child's view that the result is more important than persons or processes. Consider other responses.

3. The math specialist will lend the credibility of this position of authority to the discussion. New ideas may be generated and views shared. The disadvantage is that you are not handling this matter directly yourself, thus possibly eroding some of your professional authority and autonomy. Try another response.

PART III

Interviewing for a Teaching Position

How flattering it is to receive your first teaching offer. As a college student you have probably experienced financial difficulties, so when an offer is made in a letter, on the phone, or in person, it is indeed hard to believe that someone is actually going to pay you to teach. Perhaps the lack of pay for your student-teaching experience makes your salary offer especially gratifying.

But before you receive an invitation to join a school's faculty, you will probably have been interviewed at a college or university placement center and/or the school where the vacancy for which you applied exists. It should, therefore, be worth our time to discuss both interview situations with an eye to the factors that will determine whether you would enjoy teaching in a particular school and whether they would appreciate your teaching.

Interviewing at a College or
University Placement Center

Initial contacts by school systems with teaching candidates are increasingly being made at campus placement centers. There are several reasons for this: (a) School systems are emulating the traditional practice of businesses; (b) it is an economical way of interviewing, thus saving school systems money; (c) it permits initial screening of large numbers of candidates; and (d) it enables a school system to better focus its recruitment efforts on targeted groups, such as male and minority candidates. As teacher education programs and school systems become larger, the importance of placement centers should increase. In fact, if one looks at colleges and universities around the nation, the expansion of interviewing facilities is a reality.

Announcements as to which school systems are interviewing and at what times will be available at teacher education offices and the placement center itself. (Check the bulletin boards.) The crucial question is: What are the factors that will help you decide whether you want to be interviewed by a particular school system? (As a reminder, any interview can be good practice that makes you more adept at interviewing, and you may find that your preconceptions about a school or school system are mistaken.)

Tradition

Like it or not, what you are used to plays a part in your decision to interview. Where you were born, raised, or went to college may cause you to choose a school system nearby because you will probably feel more comfortable in such a school system. At the same time, there are many students who want a change from tradition and go to the other end of the country, if not another country, to try something different.

Expectations and Desires of Parents

Although the student does not like to admit it, his or her parents usually try to influence career and location decisions.

Many students are tempted to return to their home towns to teach, reinforced by their parents' invitation to enjoy free room and board. Other students will move across the nation to demonstrate that their parents' influence as to location no longer matters.

Influence of Close College Friends

It is rather common for young unmarried students to have their first full-time teaching experience at the same school chosen by a close friend or friends. There are obvious social advantages to having your friends in the same area.

Location

Climate plays a part in most candidates' decisions as to where they want to teach. If you are tired of cold weather you move west or south. If you want to take advantage of winter sports, such as skiing, you move to a place where you can get to snow country quickly. Do you want to be near a university to do graduate work? If so, this will influence your choice of location.

Size of the School System and the Community in Which It Is Located

Do you want to teach in a rural, suburban, or urban area? Do you want to teach in a school with 200 students or 2,000 students? You may feel more comfortable in a community similar in size to that in which you were raised, or in which you student taught, or you may wish to experience the challenge of a community whose size is entirely new to you.

General Tone of the School and the School System's Location

What is the socioeconomic background of the student body and the community(ies) served by the school? How will this influence you as to whether you choose a school? It will be useful to spend some time in the school's surrounding areas, so that you get a feel for the culture of the community.

You should be able to name several other factors that are important to you in deciding what interviews you wish to seek. The above-mentioned are but an indication as to the variables involved.

When you go to the placement center, you should realize that very few jobs are offered at this particular interview. In fact, some campus placement centers advise the interviewer not to make any definite offers. Instead, an initial contact is made at this interview, and if both parties are interested, a second interview is arranged at the school where the teaching position exists.

The interviewer on campus will probably be a personnel representative from the school system, rather than the principal from a school with a vacancy. Because of this the interviewer's questions are usually more general in nature than those asked by the principal, who will conduct the second interview. The following questions are typical of the questions you may expect from the personnel representative who will be interviewing you:

> What is your philosophy of education (or teaching)?
> Why do you want to be a teacher?
> What made you decide to become a teacher?
> Did you have a good student-teaching experience?
> What are your professional and educational teaching goals?
> Why are you interested in teaching in our system?
> What activities did you engage in during your college years?
> What experiences have you had in working with children and youth?

What is the reason for these general screening questions asked by the interviewer? Quite simply, the interviewer wants to know whether you should be considered as a serious candidate. That is, should you be invited for a second interview, to be held at the school? The interviewer wants to know about your ability to get along with colleagues, the administration, and the students. Half of the job of the interviewer at the campus placement center is to appraise you; the other half of the job is to sell the school and school system to you. The interviewer may well spend the first part of the interview talking to you about the school system, the school, and the community in which they are located. This introduction may be designed to put you at ease. Videotapes and slides are sometimes shown to impress the candidate. Slick brochures are also distributed. A major question is in the candidate's mind as the candidate prepares for and participates in the interview: "Should I really be honest or should I try to play the game in order to get the job?" We believe that your candid opinions, tentative though they may be, should be given to the interviewer. It is important that you teach in a school system that will allow you to develop those ideas that are part of your belief system. If you compromise too much in the interview, it is quite possible that you will do likewise in your teaching. The real losers will be not only you but also your students.

Interviewing at the School in Which You Are Interested

You have now been invited, probably by letter or perhaps even at the end of the interview at the university placement center, to visit the school where there is a vacancy. The principal who greets you will try to put you at ease through a variety of methods. For example, the interviewer may take you around the school where there is a vacancy. The principal will introduce you to teachers and others in the building. Questions will be asked that will determine whether you will be invited to take a position at the school. Neatness of dress and grooming, good grammar, and energy level are factors that will be appraised by the principal as you make the rounds of the building.

The cases in this section of the book should be useful to you as you consider the process of seeking a teaching position. Good luck.

7 INTERVIEWER– TEACHER CONFLICT

Interviewing for a teaching position sometimes involves conflict. Both interviewer and teacher have a good deal at stake. The interviewer wants to hire an excellent prospect who will fit into an existing school. The teacher, who probably knows little about the history and culture of the school, wants to fit in, but also has definite ideas about teaching that may differ from existing practices. A teaching candidate described the interview situation as follows: "I haven't experienced anything like this since my first junior high school dance, when girls and boys hung against different walls, wondering if we would get together."

Potential conflict exists because of differing philosophies of teaching and learning. This is particularly true, as two of the following cases demonstrate, if the teaching position is in a magnet school with a strong ideology. If the teacher feels comfortable with the ideology, there is smooth sailing. If not, trouble is definitely ahead.

Your views on gender and ethnic issues are central to your educational ideology, and this is also true for the interviewer.

University culture is on the cutting edge of these issues, whereas some school and school system leaders reflect basic conservatism that exists in the community.

The interviewer may ask questions about your interest in and ability to teach students of diverse ethnic backgrounds. Your response to such questions will probably reflect your attitudes toward diversity in general. A key to your success in answering these questions is honesty.

Case 7.1: An Opening in the Traditional School

The personnel director of a school system visits your placement center and greets you for an interview. She explains that there are few openings in their school system this year due to budget cutbacks. However, she adds that there is an opening at Jones Traditional School, one of several magnet schools in the system designed to stop white flight to private schools. She describes the school's culture (the way they do things there) as follows: Students walk silently in the halls and only whispering is allowed in the cafeteria; students' classes are not interrupted for anything except fire drills; and emphasis is on academics leading to self-esteem, rather than on self-esteem leading to academics.

The personnel director asks if you are interested in teaching at Jones Traditional School. What is your reply?

(extreme response) Progressive	neutral	(extreme response) Essentialist
No, I am not interested because the norms of the school's culture are not consistent with my basic beliefs. The students would not be able to have any input in forming classroom and school "constitutions" governing behavior, and therefore would be deprived of the opportunity to practice democratic decision-making skills.		Yes, I am very interested because the norms of the school's culture are clearly consistent with my basic beliefs. Adults should be and are clearly in control at all times, and students learn to follow rules that will lead to self-discipline. Academics are the primary focus.

Case 7.2: Opportunity to Teach in an Open School

You have had a successful interview at your university with the personnel director of a school system in which you are interested. He points out that each school's principal must recommend a candidate before he or she is hired. You are informed that there is an opening at the Alderman Magnet School, a 10-year physical structure. You make an appointment and are interviewed by Dr. Smith, the principal. Dr. Smith greets you warmly and describes the history of Alderman Magnet School. "Alderman is an open school where we believe that each student should be given the opportunity to work up to his or her potential. We don't have walls in our pods—octagonal structures housing six classes. We believe in experiencing or living the curriculum, rather than simply covering the textbook. The world is changing so fast that we must create our own 'textbooks' from the living environment that surrounds us. You will find that each teacher's style is honored as long as instruction is child-centered. We do not believe in ability-grouping because under such grouping, advantaged children move ahead quickly academically, whereas disadvantaged students are not pulled up academically by being with better students. Exceptional children are mainstreamed. Most of our teaching is project-centered because we believe that children learn by doing. We use the portfolio system of assessing student progress. We feel that a teacher who is motivated to teach in this way will motivate children to learn. Our staff-development program is strong for this reason."

Is this the kind of school in which you would like to teach?

(extreme response) Progressive	neutral	(extreme response) Essentialist
Yes, I am interested because the principal's description of the school is consistent with my basic beliefs. The school's staff believes that the school is a microcosm of a democratic society and that children learn democratic ways by living them.		No, I am not interested because the norms ("rules of the game") in this school's culture are inconsistent with my basic beliefs. Children need strong adult leadership in order to lead a disciplined life. There is an absence of necessary structure in this school. To take this job would be a disservice to myself and the school. It is best to face this reality at the onset.

Case 7.3: The Principal Who Interviews You Refers to Herself as a Change Agent

You are being interviewed by a dynamic young principal who explains her vision with regard to her school and schooling in general. *"Megatrends 2000,* by John Naisbitt and Patricia Aburdeen, and *Powershift,* by Alvin Toeffler, were very important in providing context for education in general and our school in particular. As an optimistic person, the kind of person teachers expect me to be, it is my responsibility to lead the school into the next decade. The only sure thing is change and as a 'change agent' it is my job to have a vision for the future that prepares us for the many changes taking place in the larger society."

What is your impression of this principal's remarks?

(extreme response) *Progressive*	*neutral*	*(extreme response)* *Essentialist*
The principal's remarks are consistent with the progressive position. She is forward-looking and optimistic. She is as interested in the learning of adult educators as she is in the learning of children. She is reconciled to the inevitability of change, and she recognizes the importance of giving direction to that change.		The principal's remarks are not in keeping with the general tone of the essentialist position. No reference to keeping the best of the status quo, for example, is made. She is clearly focused on herself and her leadership, rather than on the academic essentials students need. Change for the sake of change, or change in order to be faddish, is not professionally defensible.

Case 7.4: Your Response to a Speech by a Feminist Educator

You are a student teacher whose relationship with your cooperating teacher can best be described as excellent. You are like-minded on important views of teaching and social issues in general. As luck would have it, both of you are seeking jobs for the following year and think it would be great if you could find jobs in the same school. (The cooperating teacher is leaving a position in the school where you are doing your student teaching because of the need for a new challenge.)

You and your cooperating teacher decide to visit a nearby university to hear an educator's feminist critique of schools and schooling. The feminist speaker begins by saying that it is generally acknowledged that teaching is a feminized profession, whereas educational administration is not. In effect, the feminist continues, this places positional authority in schools and school systems in the hands of men. It does not make sense, according to the feminist speaker, to add on the feminist perspective, for in effect this simply reinforces the masculine industrial-age metaphor of the man in the driver's seat. Subject matter within disciplines, educational and occupational hierarchies with their sexual division of labor (men in administration and women in teaching), and other male-dominated mechanisms supporting the status quo are the result of adding on the feminist critique, rather than starting afresh with a very new view as to what schools and schooling can and should be. The feminist speaker concludes by saying that all of you, men and women, who support the status quo will relegate women to the same role that nurses have played in relation to doctors, and in the process both women and men will be dehumanized.

The speaker, a very bright, dynamic, and articulate person, has given you and your cooperating teacher plenty to think about. What will your reaction be as you search for a teaching position, and what will your advice be to your cooperating teacher?

(extreme response) Progressive	neutral	(extreme response) Essentialist
The feminist speaker is in the progressive tradition. The speaker has critiqued the present system of power arrangements in our society and correctly adopted the thesis that we need important changes in schools and schooling. You and your friend should seek a school whose principal, male or female, has a similar view of what is wrong with schools and schooling and what needs to be done to make things right. A second choice is to find a school where the principal is a manager and lets teachers handle the curriculum. However, you and your friend, unlike essentialists, will probably threaten this principal (perhaps a "good ol' boy") with your feminist critique.		This case has a clear-cut answer. You and the cooperating teacher have been exposed to a radical feminist—a progressive. Excellent teachers are excellent because they relate to essential truths and subject matter that have stood the test of time. Truth and knowledge of the discipline are not gender-specific. Therefore, you and the cooperating teacher should search for a school where the principal is also committed to the essentialist position. If you cannot find one, move to a school where you can lead the faculty and principal toward the essentialist position. Some principals, for example, give faculty members the responsibility for the instructional program and see themselves as managers who keep the building safe and clean, have good food in the cafeteria, and handle public relations.

Case 7.5: Interview Problem Concerning Pressure From Athlete

You are a prospective teacher applying for a position in a very sports-minded community high school. Here is the situation posed for you during an interview.

Danny is a high school senior who is a fine athlete but does very poorly academically. Danny has no discipline problems and has been socially promoted by many teachers to play basketball, football, and track. Danny's work in your class has been very inconsistent, a sign that he has made little effort to get good grades.

Danny has been offered a scholarship to attend the university next fall. Of course, the university is under the impression his grades meet specifications. The end-of-course grade you give Danny is the determining factor.

What is your reaction?

(extreme response) Progressive	neutral	*(extreme response)* Essentialist
Danny deserves every opportunity to succeed. He is at a critical point in life. Consider his total contribution to your class and the school, not simply his academic proficiency. If he gets a passing grade and meets the minimum SAT requirement, he will probably get special help as a tutored varsity athlete, and therefore the chance to succeed at the university and in life.		Give Danny the grade he has earned. The only question of any importance is, "Has Danny demonstrated that he has learned the essential knowledge taught in class?" You have a professional obligation to certify that to many constituencies, including the athletic department of that university.

Case 7.6: Superintendent Not There for Interview

You have received an invitation to an interview by the superintendent. You arrive a little early and take a seat in the outer office. When the time for the appointment passes, the secretary informs you that the superintendent is out and will be in shortly. One and one-half hours later, you ask what the chances are that you will be able to see the superintendent. You are assured that the superintendent will want to see you today.

What will you do?

1. Ask for another appointment.
2. Talk to the secretary, explaining precisely how you feel about this situation.
3. Leave, saying you will call later.
4. Check with others in the building, even though you do not know them personally, asking if this is a common behavior pattern on the part of the superintendent. Check this out discreetly.
5. Wait for another hour.

Case 7.6: Rationales for the Alternative Responses

1. This is a legitimate request. You have already waited for 1½ hours. However, you will have to "psych up" again and spend time driving to and from the interview. Please try another response.
2. This has the advantage of letting you blow off steam, which will probably feel good in the short run. However, the secretary is sure to pass on your reaction to the superintendent, which is a downside to this response. Go to another response.
3. You will not have blown off steam in front of the secretary and you can gather your thoughts to see if you wish to return or just forget this system. You may also use this time to check further into the system and the superintendent's leadership. You will, however, have to "psych up" again, which takes resources. Consider another response.

4. Networking is a good way to acquire information. If you are subtle, you may learn a good deal. However, you can probably count on the people you communicate with to talk to others in their networks, perhaps including the secretary and the superintendent. Choose a less risky response.
5. This is probably the best response. Your patience will be appreciated by the secretary and the superintendent. Little is lost in waiting another hour. If the superintendent does not show, talk to the secretary and ask for her advice.

Case 7.7: Your Reaction to Apparent Ignorance on the Part of the Interviewer

During an interview for a teaching position in a school that really interests you, the principal tells you about a program in the school that is in your area of expertise. In the principal's enthusiasm, statements are made about your area of expertise that are false.

How will you react? Choose from these alternative responses:

1. Ignore it during the interview, but keep in mind the principal's interest and claim to expertise in your program area.
2. Correct the interviewer and see how the principal reacts.
3. Ignore it and move on with the interview. Just forget the matter.

Case 7.7: Rationales for the Alternative Responses

1. It is probably wise to ignore the interviewer's ignorance at the time of the interview, but it is equally wise to keep in mind in the future that the principal claims expertise in an area in which you are an expert. One sign of an intelligent and effective leader is that he or she knows what he or she does not know. This is probably the best response.
2. This response will let you see how the interviewer reacts to being corrected in a one-on-one situation (which is more

face-saving than a group situation). However, it is likely
that the interviewer views himself or herself as holding
the power in this situation. Thus the response is highly
risky.
3. To ignore the response at the moment is probably wise.
However, it is probably a mistake to simply forget the
principal's claim to expertise in an area in which he or she
is misinformed.

Case 7.8: Principal Questions Your Ability to Teach
Children From Lower Socioeconomic Levels

You have taught successfully in a high socioeconomic level
community as a student teacher. You are now seeking a position
in a school in a low socioeconomic area. The principal questions
your ability to understand and communicate with this type of
student and to generally handle this assignment. The principal
intimates that your experience in the sheltered atmosphere of
your student teaching does not qualify you for the job. The principal feels that teaching children of lower socioeconomic status is
much more demanding than teaching children from economically
secure families.
How will you respond? Choose from these alternative responses:

1. Try to convince the principal that children from socio-
economically secure families can be just as troublesome
and difficult to teach as children from lower socioeconomic
levels.
2. Assure the principal that there were students in your
classes during student teaching that came from less than
desirable family situations, and describe how you related
to these students. Acknowledge, however, that students
from low socioeconomic areas do have special problems
that you will do your best to address.
3. Remove yourself as a candidate for the position. If the
principal is this rigid a thinker, you will not be happy in
this school anyway.

Case 7.8: Rationales for the Alternative Responses

1. It is certainly true that there are children in every school and school system who have serious problems. However, the interviewer is also correct that children from low socioeconomic backgrounds have special problems frequently not understood or addressed by many teachers who have not taught in such areas. Try another response.
2. This is the best response. It recognizes the special challenge of reaching children from low socioeconomic backgrounds, and yet it communicates your desire to take on the challenge. Otherwise, why would you have interviewed?
3. You have already invested a good deal of your resources in having this interview. However, if there is not a good fit with the community, do not apply further for the position. Although this is an authentic response, your desire to interview and take on this challenge is too easily thwarted by one interview. Choose another response. The principal should not be judged on such a limited basis.

Case 7.9: An Interviewer Questions You About the Magazines You Read

After several questions have been posed to you during your interview for a teaching position, the interviewer asks you if you have any questions. You ask several questions about the school and school system, and the interviewer answers them to your satisfaction. At the conclusion of the interview, the interviewer asks, "What magazines do you subscribe to?"

What is your response? Choose from the following alternatives:

1. State that you do not care to discuss this question because it seems irrelevant to the teaching position you desire.
2. Discuss magazines you have read, regardless of whether you subscribe to them.

3. Point out that you subscribe to few magazines because they are so expensive, but identify magazines that you like and have read other places, such as in the library.

4. Simply say that in this new information age you get most of your information from television.

5. Relate your view that this is a private matter and you would prefer not to answer the question.

Case 7.9: Rationales for the Alternative Responses

1. This is a kind of standard question that some interviewers ask, and they in turn tend to get general or "canned" answers. To say that you do not care to answer it, however, is to violate conversational civilities. Choose another response.

2. This is probably the second best answer. Your answer will demonstrate that you are well read. Move on to consider a better response.

3. It is true that as a college student you probably do not have money to subscribe to several magazines. Talking about magazines you have read in the library demonstrates that you are interested in learning through magazines and periodicals. This is probably the best response.

4. This is indeed the new information age, and the wise viewer of television can learn a great deal that is important to teaching. The problem with this response is that it does not respond to the interviewer's question and it does not sound very academic. Search for a better response.

5. This answer also violates conversational civilities and therefore is not an acceptable response.

Case 7.10: Your Reaction to a Controversial
Superintendent

You have an interview with Superintendent Jones, the superintendent of Perry County. On entering the room, you introduce yourself and inform the superintendent of your scheduled interview. The superintendent then proceeds to hunt for your portfolio, which was sent almost 2 months ago. On finding your file the superintendent looks through it, saying, "I did not get a chance to look at this before. What kind of a job do you want?" You respond that you have applied for a teaching position in the district. The superintendent is silent for a moment and then comments, "That's nice. What are your qualifications?" At this time the phone rings and the following ensues: "Hello. What the hell do you want? She went where? Doesn't she know we are interviewing people for jobs this week? Damn her, anyway, does she think she owns the school or something? You call her and tell her I want her back at her desk in an hour or she will hear from me. I'm sending a prospective teacher to see her, and by God, she had better be there by the time the candidate arrives. Got that?" The superintendent hangs up and remarks, "These damn administrators. They think they own the schools or something. This principal had better shape up or she'll be looking for another job."

You are handed a piece of paper with an address and a map. After giving you directions verbally, the superintendent dismisses you summarily, without rising or even saying goodbye.

You go to the designated school and have to wait for the principal to return from her doctor's appointment. On her arrival, the interview proceeds smoothly, and you are relieved to find that she is a warm, friendly person who seems to be genuinely interested in your personal and professional welfare.

After your conversation you are asked to return to the superintendent's office for an additional interview with the superintendent. If the superintendent and the principal feel you qualify, you will be notified.

What will your reaction be at this time? Please choose the best response from the following alternatives:

1. Before you return to the superintendent's office, talk to the principal about your interview with the superintendent.
2. Go to the additional interview with the superintendent without saying anything about your previous interview with the superintendent.

3. Talk to the superintendent's secretary in a subtle way about your interviews and get any information that will be useful.
4. Cancel your interview with the superintendent and interview with other systems.

Case 7.10: Rationales for the Alternative Responses

1. You are naturally somewhat in shock after the interview with the superintendent, and talking to the principal about the matter will release some of the emotional stress you have felt. This response has the advantage of letting you know what the relationship between this principal and perhaps other principals in the school system is. For example, the superintendent may leave this school and principal alone most of the time, or the superintendent may try to micro-manage the school. Either way, it is good to know this before you take the job. The downside of this response is that the relationship between the superintendent and the principal is in a sense none of your business until you are employed. The principal may also feel that you are indiscreet by talking behind the superintendent's back. Search for a better answer, although this is probably the second best answer.
2. This response has the advantage of not putting any "noise in the system" by talking to people who might pass on information that could hurt your chances of getting the job. Keep what you have learned in mind for future reference. This is probably the best response since you do not have the job yet.
3. The secretary is the person closest to the superintendent and can therefore give you inside information on the superintendent's behavior. For example, the superintendent may have simply had a bad day, or the superintendent may have a bark that is worse than his bite. However, the secretary is primarily expected to be loyal to the superintendent and likely to share your comments with others,

perhaps even the superintendent. You will appear to be indiscreet. Try a better response.

4. The superintendent of schools can have a considerable influence on a school and its principal. If this is the case, you could well be miserable in this school. This, however, is balanced by the fact that you like the principal. It is too early to "cut and run." Search for a better response.

References

Brubaker, D. L., & Nelson, R. H. (1974). *Creative survival in educational bureaucracies*. Berkeley, CA: McCutchan.

Calderhead, J. (1981). A psychological approach to research on teachers' classroom decision-making. *British Educational Research Journal, 7*, 51-57.

Clark, C. M., & Peterson, P. L. (1986). Teachers' thought processes. In M. C. Wittrock (Ed.), *Handbook of research on teaching*. New York: Macmillan.

Education code (Vol. 1). (1963). Sacramento: State of California.

Elam, S., Rose, L., & Gallup, A. (1991). The 23rd annual Gallup Poll of the public's attitudes toward the public schools. *Phi Delta Kappan, 73*, 41-56.

Elam, S., Rose, L., & Gallup, A. (1992). The 24th annual Gallup Poll of the public's attitudes toward the public schools. *Phi Delta Kappan, 74*, 41-56.

Friedrich, O. (1991, January 28). Yo-Yo Ma's crazy adventure. *Time*, p. 99.

180

Good, T., & Brophy, J. (1984). *Looking in classrooms*. New York: Harper & Row.

Hutschnecker, A. (1974). *The drive for power*. New York: Evans.

Jackson, P. W. (1968). *Life in classrooms*. New York: Holt, Rinehart & Winston.

Jones, F. (1987). *Positive classroom discipline*. New York: McGraw-Hill.

Kennedy, M. (1991). *An agenda for research on teacher learning*. East Lansing: Michigan State University, National Center for Research on Teacher Education.

King, M. L., Jr. (1968, March 15). Speech at Central Methodist Church, Detroit, MI.

Kohlberg, L. (1970). The moral atmosphere of the school. In H. Overly (Ed.), *The unstudied curriculum*. Washington, DC: Association for Supervision and Curriculum Development.

Kohlberg, L. (1975). The cognitive-developmental approach to moral education. *Phi Delta Kappan, 16*, 670-674.

Loomis, C., & Beegle, A. (1960). *Rural sociology*. Englewood Cliffs, NJ: Prentice-Hall.

McCall, M., Lombardo, M., & Morrison, A. (1988). *The lessons of experience*. Lexington, MA: Lexington Books.

Michigan Education Association. (1992). Sandia study finds much criticism of American schools is a "bum rap" and counterproductive. *Voice, 69*, 13.

Morris, V. C. (1961). *Philosophy and the American school*. Boston: Houghton-Mifflin.

Peck, M. S. (1978). *The road less traveled*. New York: Simon & Schuster.

Rubin, L. (1985). *Artistry in teaching*. New York: Random House.

Sarason, S. B. (1971). *The culture of the school and the problem of change*. Boston: Allyn & Bacon.

Sarason, S. B. (1993). *Letters to a serious education president*. Newbury Park, CA: Corwin Press.

Shulman, L. (1992). Toward a pedagogy of cases. In J. Shulman (Ed.), *Case methods in teacher education*. New York: Teachers College Press.

Steinem, G. (1992). *Revolution from within: A book of self-esteem*. Boston: Little, Brown.

Sykes, G. (1989). Learning to teach with cases. *Colloquy* (National Center for Research on Teacher Education, Michigan State University), *2*, 7-13.

Waller, W. (1965). *The sociology of teaching*. New York: John Wiley.

Author Index

Subject Index